Unfaithful Mind

By

Marion Gibson

Bridgeross, Dundas, ON, Canada

Library and Archives Canada Cataloguing in Publication

Gibson, Marion, 1968-, author
Unfaithful mind / Marion Gibson.

ISBN 978-1-927637-03-6 (pbk.)

1. Gibson, Marion, 1968- --Mental health. 2. Gibson, Marion, 1968- --Family. 3. Schizophrenics--Family relationships. 4. Schizophrenics--British Columbia--Victoria--Biography.
I. Title.

RC514.G53 2013   616.89'80092   C2013-904085-4

First Published by Bridgeross in Dundas, ON, Canada, 2013

For those who live with a mental illness and the people who love them.

Table of Contents

Chapter 1 – "I Think I Was Poisoned"

As I stepped out of the shower, my Blackberry rang. It was nine fifteen in the morning. When I saw on the caller ID that it was John, a slow smile crept across my face. Back home on the west coast it was three hours earlier and most likely he was up early excited that I was flying home this evening after being away for a week. "Good Morning Honey! You're up early. Miss me?" I cheerfully teased him. Then something happened that was so shocking and cataclysmic it would change our lives forever. With a strange and unfamiliar tone in my husband's voice, he answered me. "Mar? I am sick. I think I was poisoned. I feel terrible. I called 9-1-1. I am really sick."

"What? What do you mean? What kind of sick? What's wrong with you?"

"I have to go now. They're here," he said and ended the call.

What the hell? What did he just say to me? I couldn't believe he hung up. I was standing beside the bed with one towel wrapped around my body and another one wrapped around my hair. Staring at the Blackberry still in my hand, I stood there shocked. I was staying at my mother's new house for a week of meetings and a trade show for our family business. It wasn't very often that I was in town without John and the kids and I was looking forward to spending some quality time with my mom. She had just moved in and there were still some minor renovations happening and unpacked boxes all around the house. She had already left for work and we had planned to meet later to say good-bye before my flight home. I already had my suitcase packed except for the few things I needed to get ready. I was flying back home to Victoria in the late afternoon. I wouldn't be home until after eight o'clock. I impulsively started to dial my house number to ask John what was going on, hoping this was his idea of a joke that he had just delivered badly, but before I could click the send button, I received a text message from our seventeen-year-old daughter, Sarah.

Sarah: **Did you just talk to Daddy?**

Me: **Yes. I will call you.**

The phone barely rang before she answered.
"Mom?"
"Sarah! What is going on? What is wrong with Dad?"
Between her sobs, she managed to tell me that Daddy had gone crazy and was acting all weird and that there were police and firemen and ambulance guys all over the house walking around everywhere looking in all the cupboards and closets. She was crying, had a difficult time getting her words out and was very scared. My chest started to hurt and my heart was pounding so hard I could

feel each beat hammering in my throat making it hard to breathe.

"Okay when you say crazy, what exactly do you mean?"

Sarah explained that her dad was very confused and he wanted to know where certain things in the house had come from.

"What things?" I questioned her.

"I dunno. Just things in the house like a picture frame he found in your bedroom. He doesn't know the kid in the picture, and a wooden animal puzzle he found but doesn't recognize, also a ceramic ornament of a man and a woman hugging. He says he has never seen these things before."

John had told her he thought I had stolen these things from the neighbours' houses and was keeping things hidden in our house. He had the police looking around the house for more items he thought I had stolen and mentioned something about evidence. She told me he had asked her a lot of weird questions the day before and had been acting strange. She had had a friend over after school and he kept knocking on her door wanting to ask her questions. She finally left the house and went to the local coffee shop with her friend to get away from him for a while. As I listened in disbelief to what my daughter was telling me, I was completely at a loss as to what was happening to John and scared out of my mind for my children. Sarah went on to tell me that she thought he had been awake all night wandering around the house.

******

John

While my wife was away I began to feel under the weather, with flu-like symptoms. I was also gradually growing more suspicious about the purpose of this trip, and other trips in the past two months, and the potential nature of her relationship with some of her business colleagues and associates. I postulated that either she was the best woman in the world or the very worst. If she was the worst then how bad could it be? Talking with her on the phone only led to a confrontation as I questioned her about a colleague who casually described his relationship with his current partner as his "now person." I suggested that she should beware of such a person who appears to be, or to be creating, an air of emotional detachment. I was extremely agitated at being rebuffed by Mar, and her response and denial of impropriety was so unconvincing to me that I even mentioned it to my daughter, with whom I had never discussed such things in the past. Sarah was concerned, I think, because she sensed that something was not right with me.

I preferred at the time to indulge myself in scenarios that were more ominous. I began to suspect that the Indian mafia was part of a conspiracy with my wife and her family business, that they were preventing me from changing my Blackberry password, that they were involved in drug dealing across Canada. I had figured it out. Drugs were designed by the father of a long-time family friend who has a PhD in chemistry. These illegal substances were stabilized in plastic-like forms resembling familiar store fixtures, using an injection molding system owned and operated by one of the family businesses. They could be shipped across the country as if they were store fixtures. It became obvious to me that the Victoria connection would be valuable as my wife's role was to build clientele in BC and to trade for marijuana and cash with local dealers. Also, she was occasionally called upon to serve in a customer service capacity if there were problems. As such, several cash/drug drops were made in a day at the house, or by arranged pickups.

With all of this drug activity, I presumed that the police must have been watching our house. I supposed that a house recently purchased and renovated at the entrance to our neighbourhood was a police surveillance station. I speculated that they might be watching us, but they might also be corrupt and part of the conspiracy. I sensed that they were watching our house remotely, perhaps keeping a watchful eye on me as my wife was out of town. I thought about possible connections between my work colleagues and the conspiracy and considered that there might be some connection there too.

Returning home from the clinic, I began to look more carefully around the house, to look for clues to what was going on. This was not limited to mafia scenarios. As I found items I could not reconcile in the house I suspected Mar of shoplifting and stealing from neighbours, i.e. pictures, toys with missing pieces. There were, in fact, at least two thefts on the street involving someone entering homes in the middle of the day while people were either home or at work. I thought I had solved the mystery.

My suspicions about her grew. I started to think about other unsolved crimes in the neighbourhood. I googled the Buziak murder. I saw an artist's conceptual drawing of the dress worn by one of the perpetrators and read a description in the newspaper of the facts of the murder. I thought I remembered the day of the murder when I was helping my daughter with her science fair project on stomach acid. I seemed to recall Mar going out in a brightly coloured dress on that day, for a wine and cheese, and her coming home early. I looked through her closet for blood-stained fabrics but found none. I did find a box of miscellaneous clothes shipped by her mother from Ontario and imagined that these might be from a Russell Williams–type crime. Perhaps they were planning to frame me. I envisioned that the murder was carried out by my wife or her mother as a mafia hit to cover up the drug distribution network and connection to Indian mafia. I recalled my wife had purchased a new kitchen knife about this time and told me that the knife was special.

That evening my symptoms and discomfort grew worse. My wife and her family were aliens. I felt possessed by them. I thought I was being turned into an alien, and then I remember feeling disappointed because they had decided that there was no place for me and so I would not survive. I believed I would be sacrificed but my kids would live and continue as part of the conspiracy, alien or not. I feared that the Indian mafia would come to the house so I armed myself with a baseball bat.

I experienced hallucinatory smells and noises. I imagined that the house was bugged. I checked light fixtures for bugs, I heard a distorted version of the theme from MASH music, and I smelled acrid fumes I took for poison. I refused to drink from the tap as it was poisoned, so began to drink from a large jug of water that we kept in the garage for an emergency. I had an insatiable thirst and drank five to ten litres of tepid water that tasted of plastic. I continued to feel poisoned by water or by food. My mind ran wild. Was I poisoned by acetaminophen and alcohol or by methanol?

Panic set in after a while and I could not calm myself. I shoved a note explaining my deductions into my chair in case I *passed away. By six o'clock Saturday morning I decided to call 9-1-1 before the poison could overcome me.*

******

It was six thirty in the morning on the west coast and there were three police cars, a fire engine and a couple of ambulances parked outside my house. As much as I wanted to reach through the phone lines and hug my daughter, I could only assure her that I would try to get home as soon as possible. Maybe I could get on an earlier flight. "Are the boys still sleeping?" I asked.

"Yes. I think so. I thought I heard Sam awake but I am not sure. Maybe he just went to the bathroom."
Sam is our youngest child. He is a delightful and charming little boy who at nine years old tries to keep up with his fifteen-year-old brother, Daniel. They play the same video games and share the same interest in mythology and war. I asked Sarah to go check on Sam and then find a police officer and have him call me back. I was worried that Sam would wake up with the strange voices and commotion going on in the house so early in the morning. It would be very confusing for him and it killed me to hang up the phone with Sarah but I needed to make a few phone calls. I had no idea what was happening in my home and I was so far away and felt completely helpless. "I am going to try to get home as soon as possible, I promise you! I love you darling." I clicked the end call button, sat down on the bed and burst into tears.

Like most teenagers, Daniel slept very soundly and needed a minor explosion to get him out of bed and I wasn't worried about him as much as I was about little Sammy. All I could think about was getting my children out of the house and somewhere else. Anywhere was better

13

than being in that house without me. I pulled myself together as much as I could and called Paul, a friend of ours who also works with John. Paul lives close to us and would be able to get over to the house quickly. I know John likes Paul and trusts him. I told him something terrible was happening at my house involving the police and John and the kids, and that I needed him to go there and make sure the children were okay and tell me what was going on with John. Thankfully, he agreed to go over without asking any questions. I then called our friend Sheila and tried to explain the situation the best I could. I told her the kids needed to come to her house right away and then I apologized for calling so early in the morning. While my life was imploding on one side of the country, my thoughts turned to what could possibly have happened to John. Was he drinking? Did he have a stroke? Maybe he has a brain tumour. Can a tumour make a person suddenly go crazy? Was he hallucinating? It wasn't very long before a police officer called me back and asked me what was going on with my husband. Why was he asking me this question as if I should know? Shouldn't he be telling *me* what was going on? I wanted answers, not questions. Oh how desperately I needed answers.

"Are my children alright?" I demanded to know. I was a fierce and angry mama bear protecting her three bear cubs. I don't know why but his question made me angry. I didn't know anything and couldn't answer him. I couldn't believe what was happening and all I wanted to do was protect my little cubs and I didn't want them to see their father like this. *Oh my God!* What a horrible situation!

"Your children are fine. Your daughter is here with me and she is holding up very well considering the situation." *Situation?* Oh God a situation. Man, this can't be good.

"Your daughter said she is going to take her brothers and go to a friend's house. Ma'am, we have searched the house and everything seems to be in order."

Did he just call me Ma'am? Women in their forties do not like to be called Ma'am! Our mothers are called Ma'am. When did I become a Ma'am? Why are they searching my house? What are they looking for? He asked me again if I knew what was wrong with him. I told the police officer I had no idea what was going on with John. He was alright before I left town at the beginning of the week and the few times I talked to him on the phone throughout the week he seemed fine. Actually, the night before he was argumentative and was asking many questions about a colleague I had recently been travelling with, but I didn't want to share that with the police officer as it really wasn't any of his business. I continued to answer the rest of his questions.

"Has he been ill?"

"No."

"Does he abuse alcohol?"

"No"

"Is he a drug user?"

"No! Quit it." I yelled into the phone very irritated. "He was fine when I left a few days ago. He wasn't sick. He doesn't use drugs and alcohol. I don't know. Why don't you ask him what he drank? Please!" I begged, "Tell me what's wrong with him?"

"Is there a history of mental illness in the family?"

Mental illness? What did he mean by mental illness? Like Schizophrenia or Bipolar Disorder? How dare he say that to me? Why is he asking me this? I thought only street people get these things because they fry their brains from using too much heroin or something. This is my husband we're talking about here. He is a good man. He is a good father. He is a brilliant scientist. He does not use drugs and he certainly is not mentally ill!

Chapter 2 – Our Love Story

The first time I talked to John on the telephone, I had never met him. I had half-heartedly agreed to help my brother prank a friend. I pretended to be a girl from school that all the boys liked. Even though we were too old for such childish pranks, it seemed like an amusing thing to do at the time. Besides, I wasn't doing anything else that Friday night in the late fall of 1984 and I had no idea who the boy on the other end of the line was. I had no knowledge of what he looked like or that one day, seven years later, I would be hopelessly in love and marry him.

A few months after the phone call, I met John in person at a house party. Only it wasn't just any party; it was a party held at my own house, thrown by my two older brothers on New Year's Eve. It was 1984 and I was sixteen. John was two years older and in the same grade as one of my brothers. They also played on the same hockey team that year. My brother introduced us even though I had seen John around both at school and the hockey arena. I suddenly felt compelled to confess that it had been me that had pranked him on the phone a few months previously. It was a little awkward but taken in good humour and we had a good laugh about it. John was a big guy towering over my brothers at over six feet. He had a kind face, with striking grey-blue eyes. He had light, sandy-brown hair that was cut short but messy on the top and free of any hair products like some of those guys I knew had started to use. His skin was smooth and his face was freckled. He barely looked old enough to shave.

The party wasn't wild or crazy. No one was drunk. No one smoked pot. Nobody danced and nobody made out. We were a handful of unexceptional teenagers in different grades who were just getting to know each other, except for me who was related to the two guys throwing the party. The rest of the kids either knew each other through school or sports or from around the neighbourhood. All of us were unadorned high school kids that never really fit into a particular group or clique. No one among us was a star athlete or the top student. We weren't nerds but we weren't the cool kids either. We were simply a group of kids hanging out, eating pizza, wanting something to do other than sit around with our parents on yet another New Year's Eve.

Over the next few months, John and I saw each other at different parties here and there and even agreed to a double date with my cousin Pier-Marie-Marie who lived with my family at the time, and John's good friend, Tim, who was crazy for her. We developed a little spark for each other and it wasn't long before John asked me out. He was too shy to ask me in person so he asked me in a letter and wrote me a beautiful poem to go with it. He gave it to me at the hockey arena where his team was playing a game one evening. He couldn't play because of an ankle injury.

M
Lips of silk
And Raven hair
My beauty girl
Dances there
So light upon the floor
She floats to the sky, so high
She flies right into my heart.

I accepted and we became an official couple. He later confessed to me that it was at Pier-Marie's birthday party the month before when he had realized he really liked me. He still remembers the red party dress I was wearing and he thought I looked hot. He told me it was after that night he wanted me to be his girlfriend.

March 1985. John and Marion

Before John, I had dated only a few other boys in high school but they were not very serious relationships. I don't think I even kissed one of the boys because he had too much acne and grossed me out. Another romance lasted all of two days, and we never even spoke to each other. My friend heard from his friend that he liked me and before I knew it, we were a couple. When I told my friend that I didn't want to go out with that boy anymore, she told his friend and just like that, it was all over. I briefly dated a couple of other boys, but none of the relationships lasted very long and not one was very serious. That sums up my dating experience, three boys.

John was shy and didn't date any other girls before me and the closest he came was in a closet playing "Seven Minutes in Heaven" at his neighbour's house. Once John and I started dating, school nights were all about our two-hour phone calls, even though we lived just a few blocks from each other. We talked about our days at school and our friends, but mostly we talked about our future and our dreams. We talked about the songs we liked and even played them over the phone for each other. We told each other what we thought they meant and looked for metaphors that mirrored our own lives. John knew much more about music than I did. I loved listening to him tell me about the bands he liked and we made plans to go to every concert by the good bands that came to town. He even made tapes for me to listen to when we were apart. He really liked older music by artists like Bob Dylan, Neil Young and Janice Joplin. Not a night went by that we didn't talk to each other.

"Okay, you hang up first." I would say.

"No Mar. You hang up first."

John called me Mar, short for Marion. I never really liked my name. My family and closest friends all call me Mar, pronounced like mare, which I didn't much like either, mare being a female horse, but I still preferred it to Marion which is such an old-fashioned name bestowed upon me by my father. Ugh! What was my mother thinking?

"No, you hang-up."

"Okay," we would agree.

"Let's hang-up together. One. Two. Three." He always waited an extra second to make sure I was the one who hung up the phone first.

On weekends, we looked forward to spending time together and sometimes we would go to a movie with Tim and Pier-Marie. At the end of the night, John would walk me to the door and we would stand there sometimes for hours talking and laughing, hanging on to the night but mostly, I think, because we were nervous about the inevitable good-bye kiss. Occasionally, John would write a new poem for me and hand it to me at the door. I felt so special and on those nights, I would take the poem to bed with me and read it over and over until I fell asleep practically willing my dreams to be about him. I kept all the poems John wrote to me locked in a metal safety deposit box hidden in the back of my closet on the floor under a pile of junk, and after a few years, I had quite a collection.

Eventually, we became more comfortable with each other and saying goodnight at the door became my favourite part of the night. I still remember the feeling of butterflies in my stomach anticipating that final goodnight kiss. We were awkward, giddy and happy. Then finally, one of us would initiate the kiss and we would figure out where to put our arms and which way to tilt our heads.

My parents seemed to like John and never had a problem with me dating boys. Even though they were immigrants to Canada from a Middle Eastern, third world country, they were Christians and didn't follow traditional Middle Eastern social practices. They understood teenagers and never objected to our parties or loud modern rock music. Their door was always open and they were very welcoming to a constant stream of friends coming and going from our house, half of which happened to be their own.

It wasn't long after John and I began dating that our small circle of friends including my two brothers, their girlfriends and my cousin Pier-Marie-Marie, who had eventually agreed to go out with Tim, all began to hang out together every weekend. More friends joined us and soon it seemed as if there was always a party waiting to happen either at our house or one of our friends' places. Typically, parents would surrender the basement to the teenagers and allow them to invite a few friends. There were always more kids who arrived than were invited and our little group gained a reputation for throwing great parties.

The lighting was minimal and the music was loud. If you happened to be one of the first to arrive, you would find somewhere comfortable to sit. If you arrived later in the evening, you had to either sit on the floor or stand. Everyone arrived with an assortment of alcoholic drinks and nobody cared about how they were getting home. Of course, when the dancing started nobody cared much about anything. So began a pattern of weekly basement parties where the guys drank beer and the girls drank cheap sparkling wine and we played the music loud and danced to the early hours of the morning.

For those of us who had any endurance left at the end of the night, we would listen to something mellow by Pink Floyd or the Doors and would ride out the alcoholic buzz. Occasionally, we would head to the beach or a park for a bonfire. The town of Oakville is located right on Lake Ontario and we had some favourite parks where, even though bonfires were not permitted, we successfully managed a few and were rarely shut down by the cops. We became a group of teenagers that had our own thing going on and someone once aptly nicknamed us the Circus Crowd. The name stuck and we liked it.

The relationship between John and me followed a simple but comfortable routine. We would endure being limited to marathon phone calls during the week and then spend the weekends partying with the Circus Crowd. I continued to be amazed every time John handed me a new poem. I loved getting dressed up and going places with John. I loved the way we looked together. He was almost a full foot taller than I was and his fair skin contrasted my darker, brown skin. It was during one of those basement parties when I knew I wanted to be with John for the rest of my life.

We were at a party and it was getting stuffy in the basement. John leaned over and asked me, "Mar, do you want to go outside and get some fresh air?"

"Yes." I shouted back. "It's really hot down here, and the music is really loud!"

Even though it was raining, I was happy to get out of the basement and into the cooler night air. Really, I just wanted to spend some time alone with John and not have to shout over the music. We huddled up against the garage door and tried to get a little shelter from the overhang of the roof. I was so happy to be there with him that I didn't even care about getting wet. For the first time, John didn't say anything to me. He stared at me for a moment with an intense look in those beautiful eyes. Two lines formed between his eyebrows and he looked deep in thought. He wrapped his arms around me, pulled me into him, and kissed me deeply. We stood there kissing in the rain for a long time and I was dizzy from either the passion or holding my breath. I was so happy I didn't want it to end. I wished I could hang onto that moment forever and it was at that instant it happened; I fell in love for the first time.

If we weren't together at a party or at a movie, we were driving around aimlessly talking about anything and everything and sometimes nothing at all. We had become quite comfortable with each other and didn't need the constant assurance that we liked each other. We knew we belonged together. It didn't matter if we sat holding each other silently, or rambled on and on about our day at school. We were happy and we were in love. Eventually we would park the car and talk for hours, listen to music holding hands, kiss and make out. When we were hungry, we would go get a slice of pizza, Chinese food or a submarine sandwich and drive back to our parking spot. It wasn't long before we found some good spots and some nights we would drive straight there anxious to be alone in each other's company, snacks and drinks in hand. John usually drove me home by midnight, trying to keep his curfew, but sometimes it would be as late as two or three o'clock in the morning. The evenings never seemed long enough for us.

My poem collection was rapidly growing and I recognized John had a talent for poetry.

One night a few years later, we were hanging out alone at John's house. His parents were away on a trip to Ireland and his younger brother was already out for the night, which meant we had the place to ourselves. We were in his room, lying on his bed, listening to music and talking about our life and our future when I had an amazing flash-forward moment. "What do you see for us in twenty years?" I asked John.

"Um. I don't know," he answered a little hesitantly. "I want to finish school. Get a job," and by now he had a little time to think and said, "and be with you of course!" He seemed a little confused as if he wasn't sure if this was a trick question. I have a habit of asking many questions.

"Well do you know what I see?" I asked.

"What?"

"I see us married … with some kids—two, maybe three—and we live in a house. I see us lying in a bed just as we are now and we are happy. Like really, incredibly happy!" This was a very tender, defining moment for us, which to this day, neither one of us has forgotten. We continued to lie there silently for a long time, each of us contemplating a future together. Of course, John wrote me a poem about it.

In Twenty Years

I can't believe the way we feel
The way we laugh, the way we cry
When times are good and times are rough
And when we fall into love.

In days of late, we've been as one
Our feelings flow, our hearts are bound
By lasting ties of lifelong love
It must be so or I am lost.

I need your kiss, your tender voice
Your need to smile, your quest for life
For I am but a lonely soul
Who does not always understand.

Forever love the one we share
Is stronger than the worst of times
Is better that the best of times?
So we will never say goodbye.

We touch, we feel, we can't explain
It is yet an untried game
Our need to walk through gardens green
And look at places never seen.

In twenty years, we'll see the time
That's passed from now and will decide
That we have lived a happy life
I am glad we took the stars' advice.

When the sun sets down upon the trees
The saffron colours fade to dark
And flooding 'cross the deep blue sky
A Libra and a Gemini.

In twenty years, I'll love you more
In twenty years, I'll come through the door
In twenty years, you'll make me tea
In twenty years, we'll make love free.

Throughout the next several years, our love for each other never wavered but only deepened and we always planned on a future together. John moved an hour away from home to go to school at the University of Waterloo and now we only had the weekends to see each other. He still surprised me with a poem every so often. We still managed to talk on the phone most nights and I don't remember my dad ever complaining about the huge phone bills. He was a great dad and in the late 1980s there weren't cheap phone plans like there are today.

While John was in school doing a Master's Degree in Earth Science, I graduated university and started working for the provincial government as a Junior Environmental Officer. Even though we were not living in the same town, we remained true to each other and always looked forward to seeing each other on the weekends. The "me" in us had now become the "we" for us and we were a couple, connected and happy.

Seven years after we first became a couple, on the first day of spring in 1992 we married. Pier-Marie was my maid-of-honour and John asked Tim to be his best man. The two were no longer a couple but the four of us were still friends. Thanks to my dad once again, we were able to invite all our friends to our beautiful wedding.

After the wedding, John decided to stay in school to do a PhD. I was very proud of him but at the same time a little disappointed, because I wasn't as patient as he. I wanted more for our relationship and I wanted it right now. My maternal instinct had ignited and I wanted babies! John settled into his program and planned on four maybe five years to finish. He is very smart and a dedicated student and I didn't want to share him with school. I wanted him to start working so we could begin our life together. I was tired of waiting and five years seemed like such a long time for me. Eventually, I realized that even though it wasn't ideal we were very much in love, we were married and we were happy. I was going to have to wait.

June 1996. Graduation photo.

I was content working at my job for the Ministry of the Environment but as fate would have it, politics brought about changes and ministries merged. Before I was to lose my job to a more senior person, I decided to quit and go work with my parents at their store fixture company. I regarded the career change as a learning opportunity even though it wasn't what I had studied in university. I was curious about the company and I needed to work while John was still in school. I was happy to gain some business experience and the thought of working in a family business had a certain allure for me. I had missed my parents while I spent my time at school, they were always busy working hard, and we rarely saw each other. Then, a little over a year later, I became pregnant. John was only about half way through his program. We made some adjustments and together we made a new plan. With help from our parents, we purchased our first house in Milton, Ontario and looked forward to our future that included a baby. I was thrilled. Milton was close enough to Waterloo so that John could easily commute to school when he needed to go in, and only a thirty-minute drive for to me to get to work.

In the spring of 1994, our daughter Sarah was born and now, finally, we had it all. There was nothing more in the world I wanted. Our high school romance flourished and we were married, had our own home and a beautiful baby girl. I didn't have to wait for anything more. We were very happy.

Chapter 3 - What Happened to John?

It didn't take me long to finish packing up and get out to the car. For the end of October in Ontario, it was particularly cold and the windows had frost all over them irritating me. Note to all rental car companies: Keep window scrapers in your cars! Sitting there waiting for the windows to defrost, I couldn't help thinking how surreal everything had suddenly become. The clock said nine thirty-five. My scheduled departure wasn't until four fifteen. I needed to get to a computer and look for an earlier flight. My mom had just moved in and the internet at her house wasn't installed yet. I considered driving to work where my family was as it was our annual inventory and everybody was working this weekend, but I decided to go to my mother-in-law's house instead. I had promised my mother-in-law earlier in the week that I would drop by and see her before I left town and since she had a computer that's where I decided to go. I don't really know why I didn't want to see my mother or tell her what was happening. I have seen her fly off to be there for people who she thinks might need her help. She has been there for friends and family who have a loved one dying in the hospital. She has been there for parents who have delivered premature babies and I even remember her once going to friends to help deliver a baby. There always seemed to be something about the way my mother felt about John that I couldn't quite put my finger on. I didn't want her to know that something may be wrong with John. My mother is a complicated woman with her own issues and for some reason I learned early on not to depend on her for much.

The car windows weren't clearing fast enough for me so I reached into my purse, grabbed a credit card from my wallet and scraped the front and back windshields. As I was driving to my mother-in-law's house in Oakville, John was in the back of an ambulance in Victoria headed to the hospital. Paul called me back with an update and told me he was going to stay with John and would call me again as soon as he knew anything.

While driving down the highway, all I could think about was what possibly could have happened to John. Maybe he *was* poisoned. Maybe he had a brain tumour. Was he drunk? How much alcohol do you have to drink to lose your marbles? On occasion, I have seen John drink a lot but he has never cracked up like this before. Usually he just wanted to sleep. *Oh my God!* There must be something seriously wrong with him. John despises hospitals. He hates the smell and does not like being around sick people. He doesn't like doctors very much. He hardly ever sees one. The last time I remember John seeing a doctor was two years ago on my insistence that he get a flu shot.

The phone rang again and I was hoping it would be Sarah or the police with more information for me about John. It was my brother Rick and, even though I was driving, I answered the phone. He was calling to tell me that Maria's mother had passed away just a little while ago. Her mother had been suffering from Alzheimer's.

Maria was our most senior employee at the company and revered as part of the family. She had been working with our family for over ten years yet she and I hardly knew each other. We saw each other occasionally when I was in town for family events or business meetings. I had only been working at the company for a little over a year and my interaction with Maria was minimal. However, two days before this disastrous morning, I had spent an afternoon with Maria in the hospital. She is an only child and besides her father, there was no one there for her. I apologized to her for my neglectful, absentee family. I felt bad that my mother and my two brothers hadn't come to see her during this emotional and sensitive time. We all knew what it felt like waiting for someone you love to pass on. My own father lay in a bed for days before he passed away. Minutes can seem like hours and the days all blur together.

I had sat with Maria while she sat with her mother, waiting for her to die. We learned a little bit more about each other and I was able to help her by just being with her. I had been by my father's side when he was dying and I let Maria in on a few things that the doctors and nurses don't tell you about when someone is dying. That afternoon had brought about a new, special kind of friendship, a friendship that would see me turning to her for help not long from now. I thanked Rick for calling me and hung-up without letting him know anything about John. I wondered why my mother didn't call me herself to tell me the news.

It seemed like the last several times John or I had been to a hospital it was because somebody was dying, except for when John's friend Paul and his wife Nicole had their twins but even that was nerve racking. The twins arrived almost two months early and they were in the neo-natal unit under twenty-four hour watch. It was a very tenuous situation and the hospital was doing everything to keep the babies alive and healthy. They pulled through like little troopers and have grown-up into strong and energetic toddlers.

John's dad had died in the hospital only five months previously. He had suffered multi-organ failure from complications due to his diabetes. He was in a lot of pain and spent two months in the hospital before he died. A few weeks before my father-in-law died, John managed to fly home on a weekend to spend time with him. Three years before that, it was my father who lay dying in the hospital which may be why John doesn't like hospitals.

Maybe John had a stroke or an aneurysm burst in his brain? His grandfather died of a brain aneurysm. I wonder if aneurysms can be hereditary. Definitely must be a brain tumour. *Holy crap!* Was I seriously wishing for a brain tumour over mental illness? What kind of wife am I?

I arrived at my mother-in-law's house and parked the car in the driveway. I looked up at the house and *shit! Shit! Shit!* She was standing at the front door, arms crossed over her chest waiting for me. I leaned over and looked at myself in the rear-view mirror. My eyes were bloodshot and puffy from crying and my hair was still wet. I didn't have time to brush it out after my shower and it resembled Medusa's hair. I hadn't even thought about what I was going to say to her or if I should say anything at all.

How do I tell this woman, who lost her husband of forty-six years only five months ago that there is now something wrong with her son? I don't know what it is yet, and he called the police because he thought he was poisoned and perhaps his brain just may have exploded? Maybe it's best I not say anything until I know what's wrong with John. Yes, I definitely should not say anything.

I got out of the car and walked up the steps to the front door while trying to comb my hair with my fingers. As she opened the door wide to let me in, I could smell coffee and fresh baking, the familiar and comforting aroma of her house. Without warning, I suddenly felt dizzy and nauseous. My knees went weak and I flung my arms around my mother-in-law and burst into tears. I was like a little girl again, uncontrollably crying, wanting my mommy to take the pain away and make it better. She wrapped her arms around me and did her best to hold me up.

"What's wrong dear?" she asked but I couldn't answer. I just kept hugging her as I sobbed.

"What is it?"

More sobbing.

"What can I do?"

This poor woman who had only raised boys had no idea what to do with me. I was a girly, messy, sobbing, puddle that landed in her arms at her front door. Shocked at my own outburst, I tried to answer but no words came out. My mouth went dry and the anxiety ball in my stomach suddenly rose to my throat. I had no choice but to calm myself down and tell her everything. She made us tea and while I explained what had happened to John and answered her questions, I avoided mentioning the very real possibility of mental illness.

I couldn't catch an earlier flight that would get me to Victoria any faster than what I already had booked. I said good-bye to my mother-in-law and told her I would call her as soon as I could. I wondered why she wasn't coming with me. I was a little disappointed that she didn't offer to fly back to Victoria with me. She didn't ask if there were any seats available or even express an interest in coming.

Back at the hospital in Victoria, Paul sat with John while they examined his pupils, took his temperature, did a blood pressure reading, asked for a urine sample and ran blood tests. He had arrived thinking he was poisoned and that is the complaint the doctors addressed. Four hours later, he was back at home. There was no indication or reason to believe that John had been poisoned.

Paul dropped John back at home and suggested he take a nap and relax until I returned. Being awake for nearly thirty-six hours, John desperately needed to sleep but just couldn't settle because he was hearing things in his head and was very scared. I had a stopover in Kelowna and we spoke briefly on the phone. He wanted the kids to come back home. I told him the kids were fine at Sheila's house and that he should just rest until I got back. There was no way I wanted the kids back at home with John. He was finding it hard to breathe inside the house. He decided to go outside and mow the lawn, either in hopes of drowning out what he was hearing in his head or because he had excess energy to burn. Maybe the grass was just too long, I am not sure. He also cleaned the garage, emptied the dishwasher, re-loaded it, cleaned the rest of the kitchen and started some laundry.

I couldn't recall anything from John's childhood or from the twenty-six years we had been together that would predict any future form of mental illness. He had nice parents and a nice family, raised in a nice neighbourhood. He was the middle brother of three. His brother, also named Paul, was two years older and his brother Andrew, three years younger. He talked very fondly of his childhood and has loads of memories of family camping trips, street hockey and family get-togethers. There were many kids in the neighbourhood to play with and John and his brothers had countless friends and appeared to have a carefree childhood. I have seen photo albums from John's childhood and everything seemed *Leave-It-to-Beaver-like.* I don't think his mom did the housework wearing pearls but the house was very clean and everything seemed normal.

John told me about his cousin who had died of cancer when he was around five. He really doesn't know why his parents didn't tell him directly that she had died. He remembers his aunt and uncle coming to visit and being told not to mention her name. It was made very clear that they were not to talk about her. As a teenager, John smoked cigarettes. He blamed part of his habit on the fact that his dad smoked. Back then, parents were not were not aware of the need for protecting their children from second-hand smoke and lit up whenever and wherever they pleased. Car rides were taken with the windows rolled up, the air conditioning on and cigarettes ablaze. Children of smokers in the nineteen seventies were probably all addicted to nicotine by age nine just from inhaling all the second-hand smoke. John grew up to be a good man, just about as good as they come and yet, here we were, plummeted into this bizarre situation, very scared and worried.

******

John

I had a fairly happy and uneventful childhood. One exception I recall was that I was traumatized by nightmares for an extended period of time at the age of seven and persistently, against my

37

parents' wishes, wanted to climb into the same bed with my nine-year-old brother to sleep. The dreams were mainly dreams of being kidnapped at night from the house. I also remember one particularly vivid dream which was also disturbing was about finding a young girl's body in one of the cubby-holes at school used for gym. Reflecting on this later I have come to realize that the dreams may have been a response to the death of my cousin Colleen. The circumstances of her death and her absence were poorly explained to me by my parents. I remember asking them what happened to that little girl. I think the notion of kidnapping was conjured to explain why a child could go missing. Later I became aware that Colleen's death, due to cancer, followed amputation of her leg a year earlier. It was very hard on my parents and it had a definite impact on the whole family. My parents did not talk about it with us at all. When my Aunt Isabel and Uncle George visited with Colleen's older sister Cathy they used to tell us not to talk about Colleen. I guess we were not sure why.

I also recall being bullied on one occasion at the age of seven by a protective older brother of one of my female classmates. She contended that I was chasing the girls too much, which I stopped doing. A male classmate also assaulted me around the same time. He plunged a sharpened pencil deep and hard into my knee. We were both sent to the principal's office, I was crying and bleeding and trying to explain that he was the villain. He was disciplined (I presume) and I was left with a permanent lead-coloured scar.

******

Chapter 4 - Babies, Moving and Our Careers

The sky was clear, the moon was bright, and I could easily see the ground, dotted with yellow lights decorating the tiny islands on the west coast of British Columbia. Even in the darkness, I could see the tall trees that made this place distinct from any other in the country. We had lived in several different places and by far, Victoria was the most beautiful and our favourite and we planned to live here as long as possible. As the plane made its way into formation, waiting to land, I reminisced about all the different places we had lived, how we ended up in Victoria and everything we accomplished along the way. I was happy to think about anything else than what was waiting for me at home.

It wasn't long after Sarah was born that we settled into our new parental roles and when I returned to work found a routine that worked for us. We lived in Milton and I worked about a half hour away in Mississauga at my parents' store fixture company. John was still in school, but spent most of his time writing his thesis from home. John liked to work at night when he felt his mind was most creative. He would start working at nine or ten in the evening and work until six or seven in the morning. He had an office at the university but didn't like to go there much.

Sometimes he would go on a Friday to see his thesis advisor and have a beer or two with his colleagues. John seemed to have very few friends and didn't socialize very much. It wasn't that he was anti-social but that he was on the quiet side and didn't care much for large gatherings. John preferred gatherings that were more intimate where he could talk to a few people. I was the opposite and preferred large social events where there were many people. Our regular schedule that remained unchanged for almost two years was that I drove Sarah to the babysitter's house in the mornings and then went to work. John wrote and slept.

By the time Sarah was walking, talking and running around, we started to think about having another baby. John was getting close to finishing his thesis and the timing seemed right. I became pregnant very quickly and felt strong and healthy. I didn't have any complications with my first pregnancy and didn't expect any the second time around. I loved being pregnant. I really wanted to find out the sex of the baby at my second term ultrasound but John insisted it be a surprise. Every time I asked him if he wanted a boy or girl, he would always say the same thing. "It doesn't matter as long as the baby is healthy." Why couldn't he just tell me? Surely, he had a preference. Just because I wanted another girl didn't mean I wouldn't love a baby boy. I just wanted another girl, that's all. I wanted Sarah to have a sister because I didn't have one and always wanted one. To me, sisters are sacred and there seemed to be a few times I would have traded a husband for a sister easily. But when it came to the new baby, John always had the same answer. No matter how many times I asked him if he preferred a boy or a girl, he would always reply, "As long as the baby is healthy." *Argh!*

We loved lying in bed early in the morning trying out different baby names. John would spoon up behind me, rest his hand on my tummy and wait for little baby kicks. We only agreed on baby names that sounded right next to Sarah's name and we eliminated any name that mean kids at school could use to make up stupid rhymes. At one point during the pregnancy, I actually wished for twins and we tried to come up with twin names for boys, girls and one of each.

By the spring of 1996, John's hard work paid off and he was finally ready to defend his thesis and graduate. He also lined up a post-doctoral fellowship at the National Water Research Institute known then as the National Hydrology Research Institute (NWRI) in Saskatoon, Saskatchewan, where he did much of his post-grad research. John defended his PhD. thesis successfully and graduated. I was very proud of my husband.

We were a little sad to sell our house and move away from our families but John had an amazing opportunity to work with research scientists in his field and I was looking forward to staying home and playing house for a while. Little did we know, this move would be the start of a series of moves that would take us across the country and overseas twice during the next ten years.

Daniel was born in late October and was a very curious baby with a head full of black hair and matching eyes that never stopped looking around at his new world. The day after giving birth, I wanted to leave the hospital and couldn't wait to be at home with our children. Our family had grown. We didn't have one child anymore. We had children. There was one for each of us. It was such a wonderful feeling and made us so happy. Daniel was an easy baby to look after or perhaps we were better parents after being trained. I remember John telling me shortly after Daniel was born that we shouldn't have any more children as we had reproduced ourselves and there was no need to contribute to the world's population crisis. No objection came from me, as I imagine there wouldn't be from any woman who had just naturally birthed a large child without drugs. I think Mother Nature must wipe out the giving-birth memories from our minds because if we actually remembered how it really happened our human species would surely become extinct.

Our time spent in Saskatoon went by quickly. John went to work and I looked after the children. We resigned ourselves to the fact that, having two little ones to look after, no family nearby and only one of us working, there was not a lot of extra money. We learned to rely on each other for support, company and adult conversation. Our marriage was strong and we were just as in love as the day we married.

John learned a great deal at the research institute, kept busy and hosted his first international conference. He successfully brought together scientists from all over the world to present their research and coordinate collaborative projects. He worked hard and published an incredible number of scientific papers considering his young age and relative newness to the field. Unfortunately, his contract was for only two years and our time in Saskatoon came to an abrupt finish.

However, weeks before John's contract expired, he learned of another two-year post-doc fellowship at the University of Waterloo back in Ontario. He applied and we were delighted with the offer of teaching two courses and opportunities to continue his own research. He was appointed Adjunct Professor at Waterloo. Although this was not a permanent tenure-track position, John regarded the opportunity as a stepping-stone to something else down the road. Also, we were delighted to be moving back to Ontario, to the place where John spent six years as a graduate student.

Over the next couple of years, we built a comfortable life for ourselves in Waterloo. John worked at the University teaching and I opened a home daycare. Our children were happy and we were all doing well. Near the end of John's contract, he started to look for work again and landed a position at McMaster University in Hamilton. We were a little hesitant to plan a full move and John decided he would try commuting at first. Then John learned of an amazing and unique job opportunity with the International Atomic Energy Agency at the United Nations headquarters in Vienna, Austria. With my full support, John earnestly applied for the job and won the competition. Within a few short months, we relocated to Europe rather than taking the McMaster position. Once again, I was very proud of my husband and we were excited to be moving to Vienna. I was thrilled that I would not be able to work while we were abroad. With both children in school all day, I would have plenty of time to explore the incredible, cosmopolitan city. This was an amazing opportunity for John's career and he was able to interact with scientists at an international level.

March 2001. John at work. IAEA, Vienna

At times, the job was stressful for John but he continued working hard, published several more papers and led some very interesting collaborative research. He was at the top of his game and we were very happy. We were in our early thirties and having the time of our life in Europe. The kids were content attending an International School and made friends with kids from all over the world. We made friends with their parents. We had a few occasions to travel and managed to visit five other European countries during our two-year stay.

It was yet another new career opportunity and another pregnancy that brought us back home to Canada, only this time to Victoria, British Columbia, where we currently reside. John returned to work for NWRI, which had decentralized and opened an office on the west coast, and stepped into a Research Scientist position. They were in need of scientists and John's curriculum vitae had somewhat expanded since he left the same institute five years previously. Sam was born in early October in 2002 and although we were living far away from our families, we were glad to be back in Canada.

Life in Victoria was very different from anywhere else we had ever lived. We found the atmosphere relaxed and casual. We loved that west-coasters are laid back and we definitely did not miss the traffic and the hectic lifestyle we lived back in Ontario.

Our children now outnumbered us and juggling their schedules and activities was sometimes hectic, but our family was complete. Sam was a delightful baby and everyone that met him was instantly attracted to his charm and charisma. Sarah and Daniel were in school during the day and that left me at home with a new baby in a new city, once again without friends or family nearby.

Sam and I went to many playgroups and it wasn't long before I started making new friends, but it was an income which I really needed. Victoria was an expensive place to live and housing and groceries were more than what we were used to paying. When Sam was about a year old, I decided to open another home daycare business to make some money. It wasn't long before I had a nice little group of kids to baby-sit, Sam had other kids to play with and I was making a significant contribution to our household income. That is until Australia happened.

The Australians approached John and wanted him to build a research group to work on their water issues. Not being the type to shy away from an opportunity, John was able to take a leave of absence from his government job and we found ourselves moving to Australia fairly quickly. There wasn't a definite timeline as to how long we would stay in Sydney or how long the Australian Nuclear Science Technology Organization (ANSTO) wanted John. We didn't mind because it allowed us some flexibility to leave when we wanted. John put forth a tremendous effort to build a water group and lead a research team to deal with some of the complex hydrology issues facing the Australians. We stayed just under a year in Australia and really enjoyed our time there. Our children gained some more international friends and John added more international experience to his CV.

Living abroad is an amazing experience but ultimately we wanted to raise our family in Canada. We returned to Victoria and John returned to work with the federal government at NWRI. Upon returning to Victoria, John viewed his current position with NWRI as a stepping-stone to larger opportunities. Yet we were happy for the time being in our quiet, suburban neighbourhood on Vancouver Island.

Only a few months after we returned from Australia, John stumbled onto a new opportunity to work for a provincial organization in Alberta. A colleague John had known since his early days at the University of Waterloo told him that there was a job opening where she worked. This was just the kind of opportunity John was looking for and he looked forward to working with his friend and former colleague. One interview later plus some minor negotiations including that the position remain based in Victoria, and John landed himself a position with the Alberta Research Council.

Shortly after arriving in Victoria, John was named Research Professor at the University of Victoria and continued supervising post-graduate students.

With a generous budget, he built a lab and hired support staff in Victoria. A few years later, John was promoted to Project Manager and was not only satisfied with his work but also really enjoyed what he did and had a great team working with him. John had become a well-respected, international scientist in his field and his career looked very promising. He achieved a lot in fifteen years.

I re-opened my daycare business and continued to do that for the next five years. Then I realized my time of changing diapers was done and I wanted to get out of the house and into the real world. I loved the kids I looked after but our own children were big now and didn't need me at home as much as they did when they were younger. I approached my mother and asked her what she thought about me opening a Western Canada office for the store fixture company. She loved the idea and supported me to start selling and providing customer service to our western clients. John thought it was a great idea also. He supported and encouraged me to go for it even though I had a few reservations about working with my family. He knew I was anxious to get out of the house and make a valuable contribution to the family business.

At the time of John's psychotic break, I had been working for the company for exactly one year.

Chapter 5 - In Sickness and In Health

My plane touched down in Victoria at seven thirty-four and Sarah was waiting at the airport to meet me. She tried to put on her bravest face but when our eyes met, tears came to both of us. Neither of us knew what was happening but she was well aware that her dad was very sick. The boys were still with Sheila who was prepared to keep them overnight. Sarah drove the van knowing my impatience would make me speed down the highway. She filled me in with more details, and answered my questions the best she could. It was much warmer here on the island than back in Ontario and I opened the window to allow the cool, fresh air to blow on my face. I was very anxious to see John and talk to him face to face. The few times I had talked to him throughout the day, the conversations were sombre and confusing.

By the time we arrived at home, Sarah and I decided it was best that she stay just in case something happened and I might need her. John was waiting for me in our living room. I walked in the door and one look at John's face instantly told me something was seriously wrong. He looked different and he was glaring at me. He did not hug me. He did not kiss me. He was not himself. We sat down and started to talk but the conversation deteriorated so quickly we barely spoke for ten minutes.

"Where did we get this puzzle from?"

"It is Sam's and Jeannie gave it to us when we were in Europe. It's being lying around our house for years.

"What about this picture? Who is this?"

"That's Sage. Her parents gave the picture to me as a thank-you gift for babysitting her."

"Why are you asking me about this stuff? It's been around for years."

"What about this?" John asked, holding up a ceramic ornament of an abstract man and woman embracing each other.

"We bought it in Prince Edward Island."

"Well, I have never seen any of this before! Where have you been keeping them? You must have put them out recently!"

"No! This stuff has been around for years. Why were you showing the police my clothes?"

"I thought one of your dresses looked like the one from the newspaper."

"What dress from what newspaper?" I knew what he was referring to but wanted him to say it out loud so I could gauge what he was thinking. Our local newspaper recently published an artist's conceptual drawing of a faceless woman, in a colourful dress, who investigators believed was involved in a highly publicized unsolved murder case.

"You have the exact same dress as the woman who murdered the real estate agent?"

"What did they say?" I asked him knowing the dress looked nothing like the one from the newspaper. Obviously unconcerned with the dress, the officer had said, "This is nothing. You should see *my* wife's closet."

John had no explanation for what he was feeling and for what he thought was happening around him. He had no explanation for anything and had a hard time answering any of my questions. I couldn't help but ask him if he had been drinking the night before. He said he drank a bottle of wine over three or four hours but that was nothing. *Yeah, more like three or four bottles of wine Asshole!* I knew he was lying to me because I had already checked with the kids. I asked him not to drink any more alcohol and he belligerently insisted he was going to drink a beer, maybe even two. The phone rang and interrupted us. I answered the call and handed the phone over to John. It was the receptionist at a walk-in clinic calling to tell John that they wanted him to come back to discuss his test results.

"When did you go to the walk-in clinic?" I asked him.

"Friday morning. I didn't feel well and I told the doctor that I thought I was poisoned and I wanted blood tests to prove it."

"You think you were poisoned?"

"Yes."

"How?"

"Remember the other day when the water main broke out front?"

"Yeah, sure, I remember. What about it?"

"Well I saw the guy who fixed it. He must have put something into our drinking water. I think I have mercury poisoning."

"What about the kids? Are they sick also?"

"No. They didn't drink any water."

"Why would anyone want to poison you?"

"You tell me."

The look on John's face was unrecognizable to me. He was very serious and looked stern and determined. Was he seriously implying I had something to do with poisoning him? For a moment there, I had to stifle a laugh. What he was saying wasn't making any sense. His voice was different, his altered tone made me nervous and there was something weird going on with his eyes.

I was getting scared and wasn't quite sure what to do. He definitely was not himself. The work on the water main had happened a week previously, days before I left on my business trip. I decided to drop the issue of the poisoned water and move on to a safer topic, the beer drinking. I told John that it wasn't a good idea that he drink anything with alcohol and if he wanted to drink beer that he would have to do it elsewhere.

"Are you asking me to leave?"

"I am asking you not to drink anything right now so we can talk."

"We can talk over a beer."

"I don't want to drink beer with you. We need to talk."

"Over a beer."

"Okay, you'd better leave."

"You're asking me to leave?"

"Yes, I am asking you to leave." And for the second time that day, I sadly wondered," What kind of wife am I?"

With John out of the house, and having the children back home with me, I felt a little better and was somewhat more composed but still very confused. I tucked the boys into their beds and kissed them more times than they normally allow. My insides were shaking and I was scared and feeling alone. I asked Sarah to sleep with me in my bed that night, partly to comfort her and partly because I wanted to keep my little bear cubs close. Before I lay down to sleep, I went back down to the living room and with adrenaline-charged strength I hauled our two-seater sofa over to the front door and leaned it up against the back of the door. I knew this wouldn't stop John from coming in, but it would make a hell of a noise and buy me some time if I needed it.

I tried to close my eyes but every time I did, I would recall the look on John's face and his Pier-Mariecing glare. The events of the day were too much for me to relax and I was too agitated to fall asleep. My emotions were raw and I was scared. I was scared for both of us. I kept running different scenarios in my mind about what could be wrong with John. Each time I kept coming back to mental illness and because I didn't know much about it at the time, my imagination was finishing each scene with grizzly newspaper headlines containing phrases like "man stabs wife multiple times" and "murder-suicide." I didn't want to think these things and I couldn't help it. I never thought I would ever have to worry about protecting myself, or the children, from John. He was the one who had always protected us. He was always going around making sure the doors and windows are firmly locked. He worries about fire and had two different fire alarm systems installed all over the house. He never backed out of the driveway without asking everyone if their seatbelts were fastened. When we went camping, he kept a large knife hidden just in case a bear showed up. When we travelled, he constantly reminded the kids to stay close and counted heads. John had always protected us.

I spent the next few hours in a semi-sleep state. My thoughts eventually became more compassionate and my heart ached for John. We loved each other so much, how could this be happening? I couldn't help but wonder if this was the kind of trial brought on to test a marriage. You know the kind where if you manage to get through it without killing each other first, then you pass and you know you have a good marriage.

As frightened as I was, John must be ten times more frightened. The very foundation of our existence had slipped out from under him and it was as if he didn't trust me anymore. Did he believe something that wasn't true? Was there a huge misunderstanding somewhere? Had he been talking to someone and they told him things that weren't true? Did he even realize what he was saying? Would he wake up tomorrow and not remember any of this?

I was so tired and I wanted my mind to stop spinning just for a few moments so I could rest. I had no idea how the day was going to unfold tomorrow. It was starting to get light outside and I needed some sleep. The words "in sickness and in health" took on a completely new definition and ran through my mind repeatedly like a news ticker until I finally dozed off.

Chapter 6 - Paranoia

Without anywhere to go that night and not knowing what to do with himself, John called his friend Paul. He and his lovely wife Nicole graciously invited John to stay with them for the night. They stayed up with John and talked until he was settled enough to go to sleep. Later Paul told me everything that they had talked about and explained that John was definitely feeling paranoid and confused. John thought the police were following him and he felt the urge to lie low and remain hidden but he didn't want to put Paul's family in any danger. He was worried that the people who were trying to kill him would find him. Nicole was able to comfort John by telling him that the dog would give a warning bark if anyone came near the house.

Sunday morning at seven o'clock, I received a text message from John.

John: **Can I come in and talk? I am outside on the driveway.**

Me: **Give me a minute.**

I ran down the stairs and moved the couch back into place. I let John in and made us each a cup of tea. For the last couple of years, our morning routine always began with a cup of tea together. We enjoyed the time together and made a point of talking about the day ahead without interruption from the kids. John looked a little better after having had some sleep but still had a crazed look in his eyes and his voice was different. He was surprisingly calm. We tried to talk but the conversation did not go so well. John started by accusing my family of belonging to an Indian mafia responsible for drug trafficking on the West Coast and plotting an intricate conspiracy to murder him. He really believed there was a hit out on him. Without using the word "crazy," I tried to alleviate John's fears. I told him that I loved him and he was very sick and needed to go to the hospital. Inside I was nervous and trembling. I couldn't believe the things he was saying to me. It was as if he were relating a bad dream or a movie script to me.

"I went to the hospital and they sent me home."

"Honey you are very sick and need help."

"That's not the kind of help I need."

"Why is the baseball bat in the kitchen?"

"Because I was scared."

"Scared of what?"

"Scared they were coming for me," he replied, in a low voice hanging his head.

"Look Hon. There's nothing to be scared of. You're sick and you need to talk to a doctor." I pleaded.

John then looked up at me with rage in his eyes and said, "You know, I'm not the only one who's sick."

"Who else is sick?"

"You are."

"I am?"

"You need to get yourself tested."

"Tested for what?"

"You know what. I don't have to tell you for what?"

John mistakenly assumed the phone call from the evening before was the clinic doctor wanting him to come back to discuss the STD I supposedly had given him. His delusional mind filled in the rest of the details and he had no problem confronting me with what he believed was happening. John really believed I had given him syphilis. He was convinced I hadn't been faithful to him and assumed he now had the proof.

He said that he knew I had been having sex with many men for a long time now and finally he had caught me. He started recalling times and dates, places he believed I was having sex. He started naming teachers and neighbours and colleagues. I couldn't believe my ears. This was absurd. He told me I liked to dress provocatively and had always been flirtatious with men. He told me I have a histrionic personality, whatever that meant. He mentioned something about one of my dresses again. I couldn't believe what I was hearing. I was shocked and confused but mostly angry. I pointed in the direction of the front door and shouted, "Get the hell out of here! You can't talk to me like that. You're nuts!"

Kicking him out was the last thing I wanted to do but who knew the conversation could deteriorate so quickly in such a bizarre manner. I loved this man with all my heart. We were everything to each other. After all these years together, he thought I had been sleeping around on him, belonged to a mafia family and murdered someone. His angry words sent a blow to my gut that left me gasping for air. I slammed the door behind him, stumbled back into the living room, sat down and started to bawl. I tried to stifle my sobs so the kids wouldn't hear me. A few minutes later, a warm arm reached across my shoulders and Sarah sat down beside me and hugged me. I tried to compose myself and felt horrible for her to see me like this. I needed to be strong and brave. I didn't know what to do. What the hell was happening?

"I am so sorry Honey. We didn't mean to wake you."

"It's okay Mom."

"Did you hear what he was saying?"

"I heard everything."

I looked over to the coffee table and noticed John hadn't touched his tea.

******

John

Mar left on a Sunday and by Wednesday, I decided was too sick to work. By Friday morning, after two sleepless nights, my mind was running so wild with scenarios of deception, infidelity and foul play that I went to the walk-in clinic. I was feeling so ill that I complained that I thought I might be poisoned. I experienced intense feelings of betrayal; that Mar had lied to me about the purpose of her trip, that she was seeing one or several other people, that someone had travelled with her to Toronto, or that she had deliberately taken a short flight to Vancouver to meet up with someone and go to an undisclosed destination — I thought either Cabo San Lucas or Santiago, Chile — that she had poisoned me with un-ripened cheese that she served to me in a tomato salad on my birthday the previous Saturday.

At one point, I thought she or conspirators had a clone copy of my blackberry, as I saw a time-zone change screen come up alerting me to Eastern Time zone. I tried unsuccessfully to change my password which I attributed to foul play. At the time of the visit to the clinic the doctor listened to my complaint about being poisoned, or perhaps having an STD, or work-related exposure to heavy metals or other lab substances, something that would explain my symptoms. He looked sceptically at an ingrown hair I showed him on my leg and was concerned with the poisoning scenarios, but on my insistence and pleading provided a lab requisition for some tests, including toxicity tests.

Just as I was about to leave the clinic he called me back into the exam room and closed the door. He asked me if I had seen the movie A Beautiful Mind about John Nash, a schizophrenic mathematician, which I had, and he said to me that perhaps I had a beautiful mind too. I did not want to believe him right away but this was the first time that the seed was planted in my head that I might have a psychological disorder.

******

An hour had passed since John left the house and I was still reeling from his insulting accusations. His vicious words swam through my mind making me dizzy and nauseous. I staggered up to our bedroom and looked in my closet. I wanted to see which dress was bothering him so much. I found it and threw it on the floor knowing I could never wear it again. I saw another dress and thought that maybe that would upset him too so I tugged it off the hanger and let it fall to the floor. Then I threw all my dresses on the floor. Next were my blouses, skirts and sweaters. I threw them all to the floor. Before I knew it, there wasn't a single article of clothing left hanging in the closet. Everything was on the floor. I closed the cupboard doors. I was angry, light-headed and extremely confused.

My stomach lurched and I barely made it to the toilet and vomited.

Why was this happening? I didn't know what to do? Out of desperation, I called Paul and told him what John had said to me and that I kicked him out again but had no idea where he was going. Paul offered to go check their office and look in a few places he thought John might be. We both were concerned about John being out there driving around and agreed that whoever found John first would call 9-1-1 and say that we had a psychiatric emergency. Just before I left the house in search of John, he called me on my cell phone and told me he was in the parking lot of the hospital and that he was going to check himself in. I didn't know if I should believe him or not but was grateful that he had called me. He sounded calm and collected on the phone and he no longer spoke with the accusatory tone.

"Do you want me to come and be with you?"

"No, this is something I think I should do on my own."

Since he didn't want me with him, there was nothing for me to do but wait. I felt incredibly helpless. Paul called me a few minutes later and told me he had spoken with John and got the same message. I knew if John recognized how sick he was and was at the hospital to ask for help, I could easily forgive him; he was sick after all. But what was wrong with him? What would make him lose all confidence and trust in me so quickly? We had a great marriage. We loved each other so much and were blissfully happy together. We trusted each other implicitly and there was simply no room for doubt. This just didn't make any sense. Having enough faith in John to do the right thing was all I could do.

Once again, I found myself wishing cancer or some such terrible disease upon my poor husband. I began stacking the pros and cons of awful illnesses like a stroke, brain aneurysm and cancer and tried to decide which one was the optimal illness and which one I would prefer. The thought that John really believed these horrible things about me was too much for me to bear and as bad as it was to wish any of these nasty illnesses upon him, it seemed the lesser evil of the two. Thankfully, John did recognize something was very wrong but had no idea just how sick he really was. The truth was, he was in a full-blown psychotic episode and had lost the ability to know what was real and what was in his head.

John walked into the Emergency department, spoke to the triage nurse and asked for help. Several painful hours later, I received a phone call from a social worker who explained that John voluntarily came to the psychiatric emergency facility at the hospital, that he would receive care from the doctors and would be administered some medication to help him calm down and sleep. I was very relieved to hear this news and knew this was the best and safest place for John right now even though it would be tortuous for him. I offered to come to the hospital to be with John but the social worker said it wasn't a good idea for me to be there. John was quite angry with me. John was angry with *me?* Seriously?

Throughout the rest of the day, John spent much of his time falling in and out of sleep while waiting for a doctor to talk to him. The staff told him he couldn't use his Blackberry and they asked him to sign a document declaring him a ward of the province. This was a tough decision for John to make. He was strongly encouraged to sign the document and told he would get better medical help if he signed. Unsure about what to do, John signed the document and consequently was not able to leave the emergency psychiatric area even he wanted to. John spent the next three days in this area against his will but remained compliant nonetheless. He spoke to a different psychiatrist everyday and had a CAT-scan which came back normal.

******

John

The emergency psych ward was a crazy place on All Hallows Eve and got crazier as the day went on. There were the regular cast of characters as well as a few people apparently in costume, notably a devil with ear horns, a self-declared international terrorist, and a lisping, effeminate devil. I sat in the waiting area where furious games of chess and cards were underway, with several spectators and much conversation. The terrorist changed the channel to the movie Dracula. He must have noticed me among the others as he casually asked if that was okay by me. I was too consumed by my own thoughts to do more than smile and nod at him.

With this movie as a gory backdrop, it was hard for me to avoid thoughts of despair and death. I began to suppose that the Indian mafia that was after me was just a worldly extension of a demonic supernatural cult. I began to feel as though the conspiracy had brought me to this place. I imagined that the international terrorist was hired to brutally murder me with an automatic weapon. I watched as he drew a 9 of clubs and showed it to me and I gathered that he was indicating the amount of time I had to live. Was it 9 seconds, 9 minutes, 9 weeks, 9 months … ?

62

I wasn't sure right away but I was ready to be blown away after he went into the washroom and I heard the automatic weapon being cocked. When he returned and nothing happened, I perceived a far worse fate, a slow death.

He said, "Do you hear that?" referring to a humming noise that sounded like a loud refrigerator. I pictured a giant hidden laser in the ceiling trained on my brainstem and genitals, carrying out the task of vaporizing me cell by cell. I heard the terrorist and other patients on the ward playing cards in sync with the laser. Haemoglobin and various tissues were substituted for clubs, spades, hearts and diamonds, in a card game of my death. I could hear the conversation as if I were wearing a pair of headphones. I foresaw that I was to become a flying demon in my future life, and imagined that this was the demonic rites ceremony.

I was too scared to eat anything even though there was a stacked cart of food trays. The food was most likely poisoned. A nurse came and offered me an assortment of medications, none of which I had heard of. I asked for an Advil for my headache but she sternly replied that Advil was not on my prescribed list of what I could have. I was unable to make a choice and the nurse eventually asked me to swallow a brown liquid in a little paper cup. Thankfully, I fell asleep shortly thereafter. I recall the nurse waking me up and escorting me to a padded room with only a mattress on the floor. It felt like I was in Guantanamo Bay when I was awakened in the morning by Carl, a male nurse. I asked him if we would be going back to the hospital today. He said,"We are at the hospital."

******

Chapter 7 - Inside the Psychiatric Ward

I woke up very early Monday morning and couldn't help but wonder about John's job and what would happen to us if he couldn't work anymore. What kind of health coverage did he get for something like this? Maybe I should be calling someone. I knew I was going to need some time off work and wouldn't be able to keep up with my responsibilities, which involved customer service, sales and business development. Even though I worked from home, I was unable to put two coherent thoughts together, never mind do my job. How was I going to manage? I felt as if I were hanging on by a thread. I debated calling my mother but decided against it.

Still feeling in shock with the trauma of the situation, without any plans of what to do next, I reluctantly called my brother Howie in Ontario. He happened to be at the funeral reception for Maria's mother along with my other brother, Rick, my mother and many other people from the company. There couldn't have been a worse time to call. This was one of those moments when the limits of a sibling relationship are tested. I started to tell Howie about John and like a breached dam, I broke down and made little sense relaying the information. We could only speak for a few minutes before he said he needed to call me back because he needed to get some place where he could speak to me privately. He left the funeral and called me back.

By then I was calm enough to form better sentences and was able to share my pain. It felt good to talk to him and I didn't feel so scared anymore. He promised me he would buy a plane ticket on the first available flight and come to be with me. Equally shocked and confused, Howie became very concerned and worried for John, the children and me. Knowing he was prepared to fly out to us at a moment's notice was very comforting and he was more of a brother to me during this time and the immediate months to follow than he had been my entire life.

However, he had his own opinion about John's condition and did not hesitate to express his misgivings about mental illnesses. It was clear that he did not have a good understanding of mental illness, not unlike me, and found the whole situation nightmarish. Howie didn't rule out a brain trauma right away but his primary concern was that the children and I were safe. He can be very blunt and opinionated at times but I was grateful I had him. What was most unbelievable about the whole situation was thinking that something like this could happen to John. He had always been so grounded, strong, rational and intelligent. Did his brain just short-circuit somehow? Maybe neurosurgeons knew about a secret re-set switch in the brain and could fix him. I was worried about John being in the hospital but knew that he was in the right place and was anxious to find out was going on with him. The ringing phone startled me out of my thoughts. It was John.

"Please Mar. Will you come and see me? Just once, please?"

"Yes, of course, I'll be there right away."

He didn't want to talk on the phone and hung up. These brief phone calls were killing me. The social worker called me right after that and asked me to come in and see him to discuss John's situation. Then, he wanted us to sit down together as a group to see how John was doing. It wasn't exactly what I wanted to do but at least if I was at the hospital, I could start getting some answers. Naively I was hoping for a diagnosis, unaware that one wouldn't come for the next seven months.

I followed the signs and found myself standing in front of a large, metal door with a small, narrow window at the right height for me to look through. I could only see a blank wall and a partial view of a woman working on a computer behind a desk. On the wall to my right was an intercom with a little sign above it. "Please Push for Assistance."

"May I help you?"

"Hi, I am Marion Gibson, John Gibson's wife."

As I said the words out loud, something dawned on me at that moment. I am John's wife. I am the wife of that man you have locked up in there. Here I am. The wife. What does that mean for me now? What responsibility does that give me? Is this that moment where signing a medical power of attorney kicks in. Do I get a say about John's care? I wish I had paid more attention at the lawyer's office when we prepared our wills and discussed medical power of attorney just months before John's break. I had been distracted at the time by the Persian carpet on the office floor and the view of the city from the window. Oh no!

What if the doctors believe John and all the bad things he is saying about me? I need to get in there.

An electronic buzzer sounded and the door started to open slowly. I walked into the room and spotted John sitting at a table in the corner. His elbows were on the table and he was resting his head in his hands. He stood up and walked towards me, habitually leaned in for a kiss, and then pulled away barely brushing my cheek.

"Thanks for coming. Let's go outside so we can talk."

We went through a door that led outside to a balcony that afforded us some privacy. We sat down on a metal bench. The sun was shining and although it was cool and windy, neither of us seemed to mind.

"How are you? Are you holding up? Have you seen a doctor? What did they say?" I had so many questions.

"I hate this place. This isn't for me. It's scary here. I want to come home."

"Well what did they say? What's going on with you? What's the matter?"

"Please Mar!" he begged in desperation. "Have some mercy on me and get me out of here. I promise I will be good. I won't say anything like what I was saying before."

John's hair was messy and sticking out in all directions. He still had "crazy eyes" that were bulging and intense all at the same time. His kind, striking grey-blue eyes were no where to be found

"This is not the place where I am going to gain any clarity."

I don't know when he last had a shower and his breath resembled a barnyard. I could barely stand to look at him like that and offered him a mint from my purse. He refused it and I had no choice but to slide a few inches away from him on the bench.

"Mar please! You have to get me out of here."

It was awful to see John like this and never in my life would I ever have thought he would be begging me for mercy. The whole situation was pathetic and it made me almost wish I hadn't of come. A woman, maybe a doctor — I wasn't sure because she didn't introduce herself — came out and asked to speak with John. They went inside leaving me sitting by myself out in the cold. I went back inside a few minutes later, walked up to the desk and asked to speak to the social worker who had called me at home earlier that morning. I could not recall his name. I saw John through a glass window sitting at a table in a small meeting room talking with the woman.

The social worker and I went into another meeting room. Finally, I was going to get some answers. We shook hands and sat down. He told me two psychiatrists had met with John already and he was in with another psychiatrist now. He listed the medications John had been given none of which I had heard of before now. The look on my face must have revealed that the names meant nothing to me and he clarified what each medication would do for John.

The social worker explained that it was his job to liaise between the doctors, the patient and the family. There was no simple answer to what was wrong with John. They were hopeful that the anti-psychotic medication they were giving him would bring him back. He told me John was experiencing a break from reality and that he should stay where he was until they could get him into a room in the psychiatric ward where he would get further care. This was not the news I wanted to hear and I couldn't imagine having to tell John this. There was nothing to do at this point but to sit and wait for John and the doctor to finish talking. I sat at a small table out in the main room and contemplated the words to say to John but got distracted looking around the room.

There were armed security officers in the room and the nursing staff electronically controlled the emergency exit door leading outside. The room had the faint smell of anti-septic and stale coffee. It contained a large nursing station surrounded by glass. There were a few tables and chairs on the perimeter of the room and in the middle were a bank of eight leather recliners. A few people stretched out on the recliners staring into nowhere and a few were sleeping, at least it looked like they were sleeping, with blue blankets pulled right over their heads to block out the light. Perhaps they were looking for a little privacy and in turn, imaginably, their dignity.

The tables and chairs were extremely heavy and difficult to slide. They would definitely pose a challenge if a patient felt the urge to hurl a few chairs in a fit of rage. I mean that is what I would probably want to do if I were in such a place. In the corner, where I first saw John sitting at one of the small round tables, was a telephone and a tattered phone book. At the end of the room was a floor-to-ceiling wall of glass with a door that opened onto the caged balcony with two metal benches at each end, one of which I had sat with my husband only minutes before. There was a television mounted from the ceiling high up in the corner of the room. It was turned on but there was no volume. A vending machine that dispensed water and ice cubes was the largest item in the room and stood majestically against the middle of the wall resonating an annoying hum. There were a few small private rooms off to one side. I couldn't get a good look at them, but I imagined they were only large enough for a bed and a nightstand to fit in.

I saw a sign on the wall indicating a washroom and a shower. On the opposite side of the room were a couple of small meeting rooms, each with a table and some chairs around them used by the doctors to consult with their patients. I could see the back of John sitting in one of the rooms but not the doctor. An assortment of people filled the room: young people, old people, men and women. Some of them were dressed in their own clothes and others were in blue hospital clothing. One man was wearing a blue hospital-issued shirt and pants and had a tweed sports jacket pulled over the shirt. At first I thought he could have been a doctor until he sat down at a table with another patient and started to play cards. Some people were wearing slippers and some had their own shoes on. A couple had bare feet. I wondered if John was wearing his own shoes or hospital slippers. A few people were staring at the television but no one seemed to be watching.

I was startled as John suddenly appeared in front of me. He took the news in stride and it made me wonder if the psychiatrist had told John he would be staying a while longer. I thought he would be angry but was almost melancholy in a way. I had brought John a set of clean clothes and his hairbrush but he was not allowed to shave or use his own toothbrush. I suggested he clean up and promised him I would come back after dinner. He did not want me to leave but it was Halloween and I still had to put together a costume for Sam and make dinner for the kids.

Back at home, I called John's mom to give her information about her son. She was very concerned and tried to be supportive but not in way that was very helpful for me. I didn't know how long John was going to be in the hospital and was feeling stressed about trying to be there for both John and the kids at the same time.

When I returned that evening, John complained to me about his own dinner. He told me everyone was eating chicken but he was given some weird, red curry to eat. I suggested that maybe some of the meals were chicken and some were curry. He insisted he was the only one given curry. Normally, John loves curry but he suspected the food was poisoned and wouldn't eat it. I decided not to argue with him as he was obviously feeling paranoid. I offered to go get him some take-out but he said not to bother, as he wasn't hungry anyway.

Tuesday morning I returned to the hospital with tea for each of us. When I got there, John was in a meeting room talking with someone I hoped was a psychiatrist. It was very quiet in the room. Each recliner housed a sleeping patient. Out on the balcony, the man in the tweed blazer was practising some Judo exercises. An elderly man was visiting his wife and brought her coffee and a muffin from a coffee shop. Very carefully, with a shaky hand, he cut her muffin in half and buttered it for her. I wondered why the woman was in this place. From the way he gazed at her, I could see he loved her very much and I don't know why watching them together made me teary.

John greeted me with a huge hug and a kiss straight on my lips. Thank goodness, he had brushed his teeth! He was still unshaven but looked better and, more importantly, felt much better. Looking at him lifted my heart and gave me some optimism. He told me that whatever he thought, he doesn't think anymore and he feels stupid and embarrassed. He repeatedly apologized to me and seemed genuinely remorseful for everything he put me through and promised he would make it up to me. He wanted to come home.

Earlier in the morning, he had spoken with yet a different psychiatrist from the day before and they agreed he was doing much better. The social worker, whose name I still couldn't remember, found me, asked to speak with me privately and asked John if that was all right. He wanted to know what I thought of John that morning and explained that there were no beds available in the hospital right now. If he were to stay for further evaluation the only place for him was here in the emergency psychiatric facility. If I felt comfortable with it, I could take him home and follow-up with our family doctor and, if needed, he could see a psychiatrist on an outpatient basis. Two hours later, with a prescription for *Ativan*, John and I were on our way home, a decision I would later regret.

Chapter 8 - Making Sense of Suspicions, Psychosis and Delusions

The afternoon I brought John home from the hospital, he was calm but anxious. His eyes still didn't look right but I was relieved to have him at home. After all, they wouldn't let me take him home if he was *that* sick, would they? I didn't feel like cooking that afternoon and there hadn't been time to shop for any groceries since my return from Ontario. John suggested we go out for dinner and I was only too happy to oblige. John's demeanour was different from agitated state I had witnessed in the hospital. He was quiet, ate slowly, drank lots of iced tea and looked very tired. The kids didn't seem to notice much was different about their dad. After we finished eating, we headed home and I ushered everyone to bed a little early. I was feeling exhausted and just wanted to go to bed myself. John and I went to bed at the same time but it was a little awkward. Both of us didn't want to say anything that would have caused an argument so we silently called a truce and went to sleep.

The next morning, after I returned home from dropping Sam at school, John was sitting on the porch waiting for me as I pulled into the driveway.

"Let's go out and get some breakfast," he suggested.

Before I could even get out of the car, John was getting in leaving me with little opportunity to decline. We went through the drive-thru lane and each got a tea and a breakfast sandwich. We returned home, ate our breakfast together, and started to talk. We ended up spending the entire day talking about what had happened, what was going through John's mind and clearing up some of the misunderstandings over the last week, starting with the STD I had presumably given John. He conceded that he didn't think that anymore and apologized for saying such an awful thing. I tried to reassure John that I have never betrayed him or slept around, had an affair or felt more than a simple friendship for any other man. I just couldn't believe that after nearly twenty years of marriage, we were sitting there talking about fidelity. It was exhausting feeling on the defensive for so long and in the end, I really couldn't tell what John was thinking anymore. He was saying one thing while the look on his face led me to believe he was thinking something else.

By the afternoon, after all the kids were home from school, we started to think about dinner. John suggested we pick up fish'n chips since we still hadn't bought any groceries. It was either take-out fish'n chips or I make macaroni and cheese for everyone. We went down to the local restaurant together to pick up our order and once back at home, we dished out five portions. The kids took their meals down to the family room to eat in front of the television and that left us with some privacy and more time to talk. Before I sat down to eat, I noticed John wasn't in the room. He then came down the stairs carrying his plate of food.

"Where were you?"

"In the bathroom"

"Why?"

"I had to go."

"Hmmm. Did you take your food in there with you?"

"Yes."

"Why?"

"Um. I really needed to go and there was nowhere to leave my food."

I didn't realize it at the time but John was still in a heightened state of psychosis. He didn't want to leave his food unattended. His paranoid feelings were preventing him from eating or drinking anything in the house and that would continue for a few more days. We were getting our tea from our local coffee shop and meals were either take-out or store-bought convenience foods. John looked like he had lost some weight and his skin was looking pale. His pants were hanging in the back and he needed to punch a new hole in his leather belt.

The next morning I phoned the family doctor and made an appointment for John. We were able to get in the next day. After telling the doctor what happened and a quick review of the hospital tests, we were anxious for answers. Dr. G advised John to stay home from work for at least a month and to consider what happened to him as brain trauma. The doctor asked many questions and wrote some notes in John's file. "Has anything like this ever happened to you before John?"

"Well no, not really."

But saying not really isn't the same as a definitive no, is it? When someone answers with a "not really," then there is always the question, "What aren't you telling me?" John then proceeded to tell the doctor that around seven years ago, I had asked him to go see someone he could talk to about some insecure feelings he was having. Feeling somewhat unsure of my whereabouts and shopping trips, John had started to monitor my activities by looking at store receipts and questioning my purchases. Online, John was able to view my debit transactions on our bank's website and check the log against my receipts.

As I truly had nothing to hide, I was not concerned the first couple of times this happened and dismissed John's suspicious behaviour as his being impressed by current technology and confirming how accurate "real-time" accounting actually was. However, after a few weeks of this I became quite concerned and started to notice other jealous behaviour and actions. When John came home a week later and told me he had confronted one of his co-workers and blatantly asked him if he was having an affair with me, the alarm bells went off. My initial reaction was anger and then I felt embarrassed for John. What had he done? Was he crazy? People would talk and single-handedly he was ruining his career.

I insisted John go and find a therapist or a counsellor and get some help. To our amazement, the very colleague who John confronted showed John an enormous amount of compassion and gave John the name and number of someone at their human resources office to ask for help. John was reluctant to seek counselling and did not believe it could be useful for someone like him but nonetheless agreed to go. After the first session, John came home and said he liked Bob, an elderly doctor, and thought he was kind and a very good listener. Two sessions later, Bob suggested John suffered from a slight adjustment disorder and perhaps a touch of depression. Bob also told John that he should consider himself lucky to have me and I sounded like a good wife who was being very tolerant of his poor behaviour.

I later learned that the whole event is a typical display of prodromal behaviour, kind of like a warning tremor to a large earthquake. We couldn't see it at the time, nor could we have predicted the future, but this was a very clear indicator of what would happen to John's mental state in the future. We didn't share with anyone else what had happened and we rarely ever talked about it ourselves. As far as we were concerned, we had addressed the issue and filed it away.

Another prodromal event we experienced occurred in September, the month before John suffered the major case of psychosis. Only this time I was better prepared and when John displayed bizarre, crazy, jealous behaviour, I was able to recognize the symptoms right away. Uncharacteristically, John became very upset with me upon my return from a business trip and once again questioned my fidelity. I had been away in Vancouver for a few days making a round of sales calls with a male colleague. I missed the five o'clock departure and had to wait two hours for the next ferry. I called John to let him know I was going to be late. Trouble began when John started tracking the ship I was on by internet and knew precisely the moment the ferry docked. When my drive home took fifty minutes instead of what is usually a thirty-minute drive, John calculated twenty minutes of unaccounted time and believed I was lying and deceiving him. The truth is I wasn't deceiving my husband; I just happened to be one of the last cars to disembark the ferry.

I was happy and excited to be back home with my family. I miss them so much whenever I am away from them. Unfortunately, my husband did not greet me the way I was anticipating. I was trying to catch up with the kids on the few days I had missed and was looking for some cuddle time and instead John was cross and glaring at me. He kept interjecting into the conversation with subtle barbs and accusations. I tried to dismiss his edgy mood as his being tired from having to look after the kids while I was away.

I was hoping he would calm down when he realized that I was not late. Sometimes it just takes that long to get off the damn boat and drive home. John was relentless with his game of twenty questions and unspoken accusations and made me feel uncomfortable, and I was concerned the kids would catch on. I eventually excused myself from the living room saying I was tired and went up to take a shower and go to bed.

The next morning I figured John had cooled off and we could discuss what happened. "Why were you so concerned about the time last night and why did you keep asking where I was and what I was doing as if I wasn't where I said I was?"

"I know what time the ferry docked and you went somewhere on your way home didn't you?"

"No I didn't. Why do you keep thinking that?"

"I know you did!"

"I didn't. Why don't you believe me?" I asked and as I said the words aloud, the familiar feeling came back to me. I have a crazy, jealous husband. The conversation volleyed back and forth without any resolution until I put an end to it by telling John that he was out of line and needed to go talk to someone. "Perhaps Bob," I suggested and the belligerent look on his face made me change my suggestion to a demand.

We have never had the kind of marriage where we demanded anything of each other, but this was something I was not willing to back down about. In my books, it was far too serious and I wasn't willing to overlook it. Maybe John was stressed about work or looking after the kids was too much for him. But accusing me of an indiscretion? This made me pissy mad. We didn't recognize what was happening and couldn't possibly see the train wreck our lives would become in a mere six weeks.

John made an appointment with Bob and would be seeing him in a few days. In the meantime, we agreed not to talk about it anymore until after the appointment. Interestingly, John came home and told me the doctor said I should more courteous and since we both owned cell phones, there's no excuse for not staying in better communication. The doctor also suggested that John might still be suffering from a slight adjustment disorder and some anxiety.

John then suggested marriage counselling and I don't know if it was at the psychologist's suggestion or if John came up with that on all on his own. Once again, neither of us ever discussed these intimate, marital details with anyone. We were very private about our personal life and didn't share these kinds of things with friends and especially not family.

So here we are, sitting in the small cramped office of our family doctor waiting for an explanation as to what happened to John, what a psychotic episode really means and more importantly, will something like this happen again. Of course, it was impossible to discuss the intimate details in a ten-minute allotted appointment time and I believe we were only able to touch on the highlights. I am not sure how closely the doctor was listening or if he was paying close enough attention. In any case, he was adamant that John not drink any alcohol and matter-of-factly stated that John was most likely going to end up on some sort of medication for quite a while—indicating years. John found this shocking and began to protest but the doctor shut him down almost immediately, perhaps due to his experience with mental health patients.

Dr. G was curious and almost outraged about John having been, in fact, released from the hospital without a plan for further follow-up. I explained to the doctor that the hospital people gave us a choice to stay in the emergency psychiatric facility and set up shop on a recliner or seek further care from our family doctor. Was this even a real choice? This frustrated the doctor and he chose this exact moment to have a little rant about the state of British Columbia's health care system and how it handles mental illness.

The doctor was very aware that John needed further psychiatric care, knew the best place for him to access it was in the hospital and now that they released him, it became Dr. G's responsibility as the family doctor to find a psychiatrist in an already overloaded system. John did not like hearing news about the medication and was rather perplexed by the doctor's rant. Personally, I was stressed, scared and confused and thought the doctor needed to be out on a ledge somewhere but bit my tongue knowing we desperately needed this man's help.

This was not going very well. We were still reeling from the aftermath of what had happened between us and didn't quite know how to process it all. We left the doctor's office with the feeling of, "What now?" and drove home.

The next day we contacted John's company and filed the application for short-term disability.

Chapter 9 - The Possibility and Denial of Mental Illness

Over the next month, John became obsessed with looking for a physical and/or environmental reason for what had happened to him and spent most of his time searching the internet for possible reasons for the psychotic episode. He researched everything and anything about psychosis. He became preoccupied with a high blood-iron reading and found information on the internet that indicated that this might be a possible reason for the psychosis. It turned out not to be that significant and we began to look at every possible source in our home and at John's office for any other environmental factors that possibly could have been responsible for the illness. During the month, we had numerous doctor appointments and trips to the lab for tests the doctor was ordering. John spoke with his mom and brothers frequently that month and kept them informed of his tests and appointments.

One by one, the tests were coming back negative and, except for high blood pressure and being overweight, my husband was physically healthy. We were relieved that the tests were negative but this meant we had to start considering mental illness. This was not an option for John and he was very reluctant to ponder such ideas. We couldn't even say the words aloud in our own home. It was as if he hoped that if we didn't say the words, then it wasn't up for consideration. Desperately seeking other causes for the psychotic episode, John started to think about the possibility that someone at work had slipped him a street drug and all of this was an unfortunate, bad reaction to it. He also had Paul, who runs the lab, investigate the possibility that the ventilation system in the lab had been tampered with or was not exhausting adequately. I was exasperated talking to John about all these other possibilities and was wondering when the possibility of mental illness was going to sink in. I was trying my best to be patient. *In sickness and in health.*

One evening John became fixated with an area on our kitchen floor. We had re-done the floor ourselves a few years previously and, as bad home renovations usually go, there was an uneven spot left in the floor that we didn't know how to get rid of. You couldn't see where the spot was, but if you stepped on it just right, you could feel it. Now he couldn't feel it or find it. John was positive that I had secretly hired a carpenter to come in and fix it while he was at work. I told him the spot was still there but he was convinced it wasn't. John called the kids to come and look at it but they seemed a little indecisive. They wouldn't say yea or nay and this irritated John so much he continued with the inquisition. When he went into the crawlspace looking for sawdust or evidence, I got worried. Not because he was going to find anything but because I was worried that, in his delusional mind, he was going to make something up to prove his point. It would likely be something I wouldn't be able to defend. I was catching on to how this illness was manifesting. It seemed to be taking on a personality all of its own.

Months later John confessed to me that a few times he left his Blackberry recording while he left the house to run errands or pick-up one of the kids from school. He was trying to record me on the phone with a secret boyfriend or inviting a lover over for a quickie. He was still paranoid and suspicious of me at this point and had a hard time trusting me. I was suspicious of him and had a hard time trusting him. The situation was tense and the atmosphere in the house was dark. I was trying my best to keep things normal for the sake of the kids and felt the constant need to buffer John's erratic behaviour from the kids. I wasn't sleeping very well because I was so worried about everything and simple things like making dinner became a burden for me. We had no idea how bad things were going to become over the next couple of months.

Howie continued to be my confidant and he always made himself available for me. However, he still couldn't give me the right kind of support and friendship I needed. I needed somebody else to talk to. I needed another woman. Once again, I briefly contemplated phoning my mother and decided against it. We just didn't have the kind of bond that would allow me to confide in her. I always suspected that she didn't care for John as much as she said she did. She never said anything openly antagonistic directly to him, but did say things to me that made me question her true feelings about my husband.

Eventually, I decided to confide in Maria from the company. There was something about her that day in the hospital when her mother was dying that made me feel I could trust her. My instincts told me she was a good person.

The guilt of being unable to work was eating away at me. I wanted to ask for a leave of absence, Maria was the person who was able to grant it to me and I had to believe she would keep the reason confidential. I wasn't ready to let the rest of my family know about John's situation yet, and I was beginning to feel backed into a corner. Something had to give. I felt I could trust her and expected that she would respect our privacy.

Talking with Maria was the best thing I could have done at that point. After I told her the situation, she told me not to worry about my job and responsibilities; she and Howie could easily cover for me. She took the pressure off and reminded me that over the years, the company and the owners, being my parents, had done far more for employees in less dire situations. Even though it wasn't necessary, I asked her not to tell my mother and told her Howie knew everything. It wasn't long before both Howie and Maria became my sounding boards and provided me with the strength and support I desperately needed.

Maria is a very good listener. Howie, not so much. Sometimes all I needed was someone to listen to me and give me an opportunity to unload the burden of all the craziness. They made it possible for me to spend my time figuring out things without the stress of worrying about work and I was able to focus on John. Most of all, they respected our privacy and made themselves available for me to talk to them whenever I needed.

However, their main concern always focused around our safety and they both felt rather helpless being so far away. Maria had a little more experience and understanding about mental illness. She never openly spoke about violence but always tried to warn me that unpredictable things could happen. She always reminded me to be careful in a genuine and caring way. Maria also knew I was all alone out west and didn't have anyone to help me. She urged me to tell my mother. When I explained to her our complicated relationship, she respected my decision but also said my mom might surprise me.

I wasn't ready to take that chance. My brother Rick had recently done something terrible that disappointed all of us and my mother was preoccupied with that situation. She spent an unhealthy amount of time and energy, devoted to my brother. She was constantly making excuses for his shortcomings and addictions, desperately trying to protect him, and I felt she was not really available for me.

Sometime around the middle of the month, about two weeks after John came home from the hospital we received a phone call from a social worker from Children and Family Services. He wanted to come to our home and ensure that we had a satisfactory safety plan in place to protect the kids in the event that something similar should happen again. He also informed us that John was not to be alone with the kids until his doctor was confident that he was well again.

This was a very difficult moment for John. It was tough for him to have to listen to another man come into our home and tell him he was not fit to be alone with his own children. We both understood why this was required but nonetheless it was very challenging for John. He looked sad and defeated that day. This new stipulation imposed on us didn't seem to be too problematic except when it came time to go dress shopping for Sarah's winter prom. We had to tote John along with us and he did not like shopping. Period.

We girls were a little disappointed because we were not going to get the day we had been planning for months. We had been looking forward to a leisurely girly day of shopping, lunching and more shopping. We wanted to look at shoes, purses and other accessories. Sarah was planning to move to Ontario in the fall to go to university and this day was meant to be a *Hallmark* moment for mother and daughter. We had to rethink the situation and make the most of it so we mapped out a shortened version of the day that didn't include lunch and headed straight to our few favourite stores in more of a power shop mode. We would save the shoe and accessory shopping for another time.

We knew John wouldn't have the patience for that kind of shopping. I felt a little sad for Sarah and spent a brief moment mourning my own *Hallmark* moment, but in the end the shopping trip turned out pretty good. By the fourth store and only two hours later, we had found a perfect dress. I was so proud of Sarah for not complaining about her dad coming along and being able to accept the situation for what it was. While she swayed to and fro in front of the three-way mirror, admiring herself in this dress from every possible angle, I could see she possessed all the poise and grace she needed to carry herself throughout her life.

Things were just beginning for her. More importantly, she was a kind and compassionate young woman and we always told our kids, smarts and good looks will only take you so far, but kindness will ensure your successes. I had the urge to pat ourselves on the back because at that moment I knew we had done a great job raising her and wouldn't have to worry about her once she left home. Seeing her standing in front of the full-length mirror at the dress store, I looked past the dress and saw a very bright, mature and capable young woman. I then looked over at John sitting in a chair off to the side and hoped he saw the same thing.

One evening a few days after the shopping trip, when the kids had gone to bed, Delusional John confronted me and said he knew I was pregnant. I told him, I wasn't pregnant and asked him why he thought this. It's a good thing I am not sensitive about my weight. Sure, I'd like to lose some pounds but I suspected we were talking about something a little more involved here. John insisted I had the look of a pregnant woman and insisted he could see signs that I might not recognize. He wanted to go buy a pregnancy test. I was appalled and irritated because there is no way he could know I was pregnant before I would know, yet he was being very persistent and damned irritating. He was determined to make me take a test. I was mad and refused to indulge him and this made him mad.

I finally agreed to do it in the morning but he would have to go buy the test, and I chastised him that it was a waste of money. He said he would wait since I was so opposed to the idea of taking a test and figured time would tell soon enough. I quit arguing with him and we let the matter drop for the time being. I was hopeful that he would move on to something else. I knew I wasn't pregnant since I was in the middle of my period. I just wasn't going to let him know that. It was rather immature of me, I know!

Amongst the numerous doctor appointments and trips to the lab, we also made an appointment to go and see Bob, John's psychologist. We initially saw Bob together and told him about the psychotic episode, the hospitalization, the psychiatric assessment, the tests and everything going on in John's head. Bob was surprised that something like this could happen to John and admitted he didn't see it coming. He seemed rather perplexed and was very accommodating for future appointments. He suggested we meet again a few times and try to find the underlying cause of this unexpected situation. However, he did not offer up any sort of diagnosis and I was left feeling unsatisfied and disappointed that we weren't closer to any answers or even an explanation beyond, "The human brain is very complex."

By the end of the month, after all the appointments were over, there wasn't much for us to do but wait. John had been to numerous appointments with the family doctor and the psychologist. He had been poked and prodded from top to bottom. *He had an ECG and had his prostate examined.* He peed in jars, pooped on sticks and offered up vials of blood. We waited for results, waited for the next appointment, waited for someone to call. Waited for a psychiatrist. Waited for our lives to start again. I am not exactly sure what we were waiting for but that is how we seemed to be spending most of our time.

During all this sitting around and waiting, there was plenty of time to talk. We talked about our marriage, our relationship, our kids and our life together. We talked about the past, our future, the kids' futures and future renovations. The atmosphere grew a little lighter and we seemed to work through some of the issues. Deep down inside, I think John knew there was really nothing physically wrong with him. He was feeling stronger, healthier and a little more settled. He was anxious to get back to work and put the events of the last month behind him.

He was fed up with being at home, bored and in partial denial about mental illness. He didn't think he was currently suffering from a mental illness but might have had something called "a brief psychotic episode" where it can happen once to a person and never happen again. He was willing himself better and just wanted to get back to normal.

We actually reached the point where we could joke about what happened. "I think my cheese slid off my cracker!" John would say, or "I went a little nutsy-Fagan there!" We had grown closer and felt more bonded and together than we had in a long time. Some days it was like being on vacation after the kids went to school. We would sometimes go back to bed and lounge around for hours. We would go out for lunch and grocery shopping together, something new for John.

One Saturday afternoon, we dropped Sam at a birthday party at the other end of town and had a few hours to kill. We ended up at a furniture store and started looking at bedroom suites. We were tired of our bedroom looking like something that resembled a student's dorm room. Our night side tables were TV stands and we shared a dresser. I was a little hesitant at first, spending such a large amount of money, but at the same time excited at the prospect of the new furniture. After all, we had been married almost twenty years and didn't we deserve nice new furniture after all this time? I felt bad about doing this but I had to question John about whether this was a guilt purchase. I asked him if the only reason he wanted to buy new furniture was because of everything that happened and he somehow wanted to make it up to me. He assured me it wasn't and that he thought it was about time we bought something nice. So right then and there, we spontaneously purchased a new bedroom suite.

The furniture shopping became a little contagious and got us looking at new living room furniture. With all that sitting around, we realized that our couch was very uncomfortable and the springs were poking out. Maybe we should have thought about the living room before purchasing the bedroom. I was sceptical at first but John was certain we could afford it and we started looking at new couches and chairs also. I was just happy to get off the uncomfortable couch at home and get out of the house.

John was obviously feeling better because before he would never want to spend any kind of money if he wasn't feeling good about things. We were feeling optimistic that whatever had happened was finished and there was no reason anything like that should happen again. Before John could return to work, he needed to go back to the family doctor, discuss the results for a final check-up and get a note declaring him fit and able with a clean bill of health and that he was well enough to go back to work. His appointment was in a few days and we were feeling positive and expecting an all clear.

Chapter 10 - Did You Say Divorce?

I had just finished cleaning the bathroom and came down the stairs as John was walking up the driveway after his appointment with Dr. G. He came into the house and went straight up to the bathroom. A minute later, he sat down on the uncomfortable loveseat that matched the uncomfortable couch and I couldn't read the unfamiliar expression on his face.

"I know what you do in this house while I am not here."

"What?" I said thinking he was being playful.

"When I am at work and no one is here. I know what you are doing."

"Well do you now?" Trying to sound coy.

"Just confess. I know what you do."

"What? Wait a minute. I am not sure we are talking about the same thing." The *Family Ties* theme song playing in my head came to a record-player-needle-type screeching halt.

"Exactly what do you think I do here when you're not home?" I asked John directly and sternly.

We argued for about ten minutes until I phoned Dr. G's office and asked to come right back. The doctor invited us into the exam room and asked what the problem was. I explained to him that the minute John returned from his appointment, he came home and accused me of having sex with a city worker in our bathroom. The doctor asked me to leave the room to talk to John privately. I returned to the waiting room with tears streaming down my face. There was an older woman and another man, who didn't look like her husband, also sitting there. I must have made them uncomfortable because they were trying to look anywhere but at me. I just couldn't stop crying. A few minutes later, the doctor came out, asked John to sit in the waiting room and brought me in to talk to him. He asked me why so many tears? *Hell-o!* Didn't he hear me the first time? City worker. Sex in the bathroom? I told him that while John was here supposedly getting a clean bill of health he came home and thought I was getting busy in my bathroom. Did he really need to ask?

"Well were you?"

"NO!"

Then together back in the exam room Dr. G gave us a choice. "Okay John. I believe your wife's story and I don't believe yours. You are seriously ill and either you agree to take the medication I prescribe for you right now or I'll have to call somebody and the men in white coats are going to come and take you to the hospital. I'll give you and your wife a few minutes to discuss this privately and come back in." John was terrified of the hospital and the experience he already had there so he was very quick to agree to the medication and there was no time or discussion needed to make the decision. The doctor left the room and came back seconds later with some little boxes containing an anti-psychotic medication called *Abilify*. He started John on two milligrams and said after one week to up the dosage to five milligrams. He explained to John that he would be ramping up the dosage every few days until the delusions were gone. He also prescribed a blood pressure pill for John called Coversyl to be taken daily.

Over the next few weeks John diligently followed the doctor's prescribed plan and gradually increased the *Abilify* dosages. The delusions continued even though John was taking fifteen milligrams of the medication. At first, John believed I had sex with the doctor on the very day he went on the medication and it took some convincing to make him believe otherwise. Then he accused me several times of having sex with grocery store employees while we were shopping together at the store. If I left the checkout to get a forgotten item, he thought I was slipping away for a quickie. Once I needed to go the bathroom and apparently it was fast sex I was after. He began to accompany me on every grocery trip because he was sure I was having sex with strangers.

The delusions were relentless and there was no predicting what was coming next. Every man was suspect: delivery guys, the mail carrier, neighbours. I couldn't escape the accusations. When we went back to the furniture store to buy the couch we finally chose, he accused me of seducing the furniture sales man into sex because apparently asking if there was a water cooler around was code for promiscuous sex.

John believed I was sleeping with men whenever and wherever I could. He said that I dressed very provocatively and acted flirtatious wanting attention from men. Again he told me I had a histrionic personality.

"A Histri – what? What does that even mean?"

"It means you want and crave attention and you will do anything to get it."

After a month had passed John was taking twenty milligrams of *Abilify* but the delusions continued. I wanted him to go back to the doctor but he didn't want to. In his mind, I was the roving whore of the neighbourhood who belonged to an Indian mafia family trying to murder him by poisoning his food. I was worn down and didn't know how much longer I could continue like this.

Howie continued to be supportive and promised me he would come as soon as I gave him the word. He was very worried for me and feared for my safety. He also reminded me that John was sick and this wasn't his fault. He reassured me that John loved me and it was the illness talking, not my husband. The reality of the situation was we had no idea of how stable John really was and there was an underlying fear that he could get violent with the kids or me at any time. Howie and I talked on the phone every day and every day he was shocked and astonished at the extent and the nature of the delusions. What was happening to my life?

One afternoon while out Christmas shopping together, John found Jesus. He suddenly became overjoyed and elated.

"I know what our purpose on Earth is."

"Do you now?" I asked.

"Yes. I've figured it out. I know why we are here."

He looked over at me from the passenger seat and beamed. If I hadn't been so traumatized, I would have thought he looked beautiful.

"We are here to serve one person. To get to know them and make them happy and do everything we can for them. Our purpose is to love them completely."

"Really? And I suppose you figured out who that person is then?"

"Yes! You of course. I am going to make you happy. I love you so much. That is my purpose on this Earth."

"Okay then. I am glad you figured it out."

John was so sincere and seemed so repentant. He apologized for being so much trouble, promised me that it was all over, and told me how much he loved me and needed me.

John's mom spoke with him a couple of times during this period. She always told him to behave himself and warned him to be good, as if he had a choice about what he was doing. The few times I spoke with her and told her some of the things that were happening, she would just agree that he was ill and should listen to the doctor and to continue to take the medicine. "You're doing the right thing," she would say. I could sense it was difficult for her to hear the gruesome details.

John's younger brother Andrew was supportive and told me that he loved me, believed me and knew I couldn't possibly do the things John was accusing me of. "He's definitely sick Mar. You need to get to the bottom of it." I was scared for John, for me and for the kids and wondered how much longer this could go on? I begged John to go back to the doctor and John kept begging me to confess. He was convinced he was onto something. Then he would apologize and tell me he didn't believe those things anymore.

Something had to give. I was so tired of being on the defensive and I desperately wanted to have our life back. I was tired of crying myself to sleep every night and waking up in tears every morning. This was like a very scary rollercoaster and I wanted off. I wanted to be happy again. I missed being happy.

A few days later, John searched through my desk. He told me that all the business cards on my desk were my trophies and now he knew what my business meetings were all about.

"You do you realize half those cards are from women, don't you?" I asked him and then he replied, "Well you like it anyway you can get it, don't you?"

"Not only are you sick but you're an asshole too!" I screamed back at him.

Just when I thought things couldn't get any worse, John decided to go through my dirty laundry. He told me he found evidence in my underwear of my infidelity and he finally had the proof he was looking for. I think this was my absolute lowest moment yet. Who was this man and what had he done with my husband? How could we go on? I was feeling helpless, alone and isolated. I lost hope and was afraid of the future. I feared for my kids and had no idea how to tell them what was happening. This crushed my soul.

One evening John was particularly agitated and questioned my fidelity right from the beginning of our marriage. He was asking about things that had happened over twenty years previously. He asked questions about my previous boyfriends and had questions about boys who were just my friends. He wanted me to recall specific events, conversations, places and times. It came down to a terrible banter of I said, you said, he said, she said.

I began to make a list. A real list on which I wrote down the name of every person John thought I had either slept with or wanted to sleep with. I thought that the doctor might be interested in reading the list. It consisted of over thirty men that included every neighbour, male teacher, deliveryman, grocery clerk and friend. It was nuts! There was no point to it. I couldn't defend myself and felt I really shouldn't have to. Why was I trying to defend myself against an imaginary list of infidelities? It wasn't real. Misgivings about our relationship and fidelity had never been something we had to contend with, ever!

"I want a divorce." He said to me. Inside I was screaming. He wanted a divorce! I couldn't believe he said that. I didn't think it was possible for anything to shock me now. I believed I had heard it all, but I was wrong. Asking for a divorce was more than I could stomach. I knew he was sick and I wanted to believe he didn't mean what he was saying but I was completely stunned. The bittersweet irony left me speechless. I was fighting to keep us together so I could help him get well and he wanted a divorce. I loved him so much. He said it again only this time he spoke with such strong conviction it made me shudder. I really didn't know what to say. Oh damn! He was serious. Up to now, I naively believed that our love was stronger than this and we could work through it. I thought our bond was unbreakable. Evidently, not so.

"Fine!" I yelled back and was only too happy to oblige.

John then went on to tell me he had it all figured out. He was going to keep the house and pay me off. He would continue to provide for the kids but not me. He was sure he could prove in court that I had been unfaithful and broken our marriage vows. He spat out figures and numbers and narrowed it down to a final figure. *Oh crap! What am I going to do?*

Chapter 11 - A Broken Woman

The delusions were coming fast and furious. Faster than I could keep up. Each time it was like a blow to the gut with cannonball force. The *Abilify* simply wasn't working. Then things deteriorated even more if that was even a possibility. John decided to question the paternity of the kids and demanded DNA tests on all three of them. He was angry, he was loud and the kids heard him. I was full of despair and sorrow. Could this really be the end for us? How could I ever fix this and explain to the kids what had happened? I didn't know what to do anymore. I had no idea what to say.

I indulged John, which I later learned I should never have done, and agreed to do whatever he wanted. Blood tests. Lab of his choice. Doctor. Nurse. Even if the tests were performed and the paternity of the children were confirmed, Delusional John wouldn't have believed them anyway, but part of me, the desperate part, believed that if I could just prove one thing I could convince John that he was delusional.

I asked him if we had the tests done and they proved the paternity of the children if would he go back to the hospital for help. I desperately wanted him to agree to this but he wouldn't deal. He was adamant that we go to the lab of his choice, and when I agreed to do what he wanted, he got distracted by yet more delusions and in an instant I was a promiscuous, provocatively dressed, whore again. This really pushed me down and I got furious. I reached my breaking point and told him he had to leave now. "You are sick and you need help. Now get the hell out!" I screamed at him and pointed to the door. I didn't care anymore. I was a broken woman. I had no idea if he was going to leave and for a moment, he just sat there in the chair.

The doctor scolded me later that you don't turn a mentally ill patient out onto the street. Well what did I know? John got up without saying a word and went upstairs. He came down a few minutes later with a small suitcase and walked over to the front door. He turned around, looked at me with crazy eyes and left the house. I was shaking, scared and mildly relieved. I had no idea where he was headed nor did I care very much at that moment. The person I fell in love with was gone and left a big jerk in his place.

Living with John at this point was like living with a jack-in-the-box, waiting for it to pop up at any moment only to start the delusional cycle all over again. John phoned me later that night and told me he was staying at a hotel. I was glad I knew where he was but had no interest in talking to him and urged him to go back to the hospital. He said he didn't need to go back to the hospital and he wanted time to think.

He spent the next day alone in his room and spoke with each of his brothers a few times on the phone. Paul, John's older brother, felt sorry for him and suggested that he fly home to Ontario to be with family. Paul knew John needed someone to talk to and couldn't bear the thought of John being all alone. John phoned me that night and told me he was getting on a plane in the morning and going to his mother's home. I knew this would be a huge mistake. I begged him to come back.

I had called the Crisis Line and learned that Victoria has an emergency mental health team that will come out to your home if necessary and help resolve any conflicts or make a recommendation for treatment. John did not want to come home. I also learned that it is very dangerous for a delusional person to travel far from home and especially fly. It takes them away from their support people and their doctors. The added stress of flying can also agitate a psychotic person and make them unpredictable.

I contemplated calling the airline or the police or someone who would listen to me, to tell them a crazy person was getting on one of their planes and to stop him. I didn't follow through and thought it might be a good thing for his family to see him like this. Maybe they would start believing me and do something helpful. But John's family did not contact me. They did not want to talk to me. John did not want to come back home. He had booked a flight and was adamant that he was leaving town and leaving me. I was devastated.

The next morning I phoned John's mom to see if she knew that John was on his way. She told me it was Paul's idea and didn't seem that interested in talking to me. I told her John asked for paternity tests for the children. She told me she didn't want to get in the middle of any marital issues. You've got to be kidding me! I had to gather every ounce of strength I had left in me to be polite. I reminded

105

her that it was very important that John not have any alcohol. "Don't even have it in the house," I pleaded. I stressed the importance that he stay on his medication. I was still hopeful that it was going to kick-in at any moment now. I asked her to call me when she had a chance just to tell me that he arrived. I didn't even know whether to believe John when he said he was going to get on a plane. She agreed not to have any alcohol in the house and said she would make sure he took his medication.

I went to see Dr. G as soon as I could and told him all about the delusions and that John had left town and had gone to be with his family. He was very concerned and wanted John on the highest dose of *Abilify* at thirty milligrams as soon as possible. He offered to write a script for John and fax it to the pharmacy in Oakville where his mother lives. They could pick it up so he could start taking it right away. He also gave me a copy in case John decided to return.

The doctor also pointed out to me that families have an uncanny ability to protect their own so not to expect much to happen. When I suggested the dosage change to John, he got very upset and laughed me off. Paul got on the phone and said that he wondered how a doctor could write a prescription for a patient without even seeing him. Paul also didn't think that John seemed that bad and thought a few days at home around family would give us some time to "cool off." Seriously? My mother-in-law took her sons out for dinner and the two boys ordered beers.

I found out that John's mom also bought beer for the house. Were they all effing delusional? My mother-in-law did call me back later that night to let me know he seemed all right and looked fine. She said she was going to bed and leaving her two sons alone to talk. I appreciated her calling but wished she had said more. She never addressed the paternity tests or offered me any sort of comfort or compassion.

Feeling desperate, I wanted John's family to see what was happening for real and meet Delusional John, the one I had been living with for the past several months. I told John that two men came to deliver and set-up the new bedroom furniture hoping this would set him off on a rant.

"What did they have to do?"

"They had to remove the packaging and screw the handles on. It took them a while. They were up in the bedroom quite a while but everything looked nice when they were done." I tried to agitate John so that he would get angry with me and let his smokescreen down. I wasn't successful. I am not sure if his family was in the room with him listening to us nor do I know what happened after he hung up but he took the bait, taunted me and replied that I probably li-i-ked it. He wanted to know exactly how long they were working and how many handles were installed. I know now that was not a very nice thing to do but I was desperate and felt I had no other choice. I needed them to see what was really going on with John.

It took me three days to gain any interest in straightening up the bedroom, getting the furniture put in the right place and transferring our clothes from the old dresser to the new ones. I couldn't get happy about the furniture if I couldn't share the excitement with John. For almost twenty years, we waited to buy ourselves a bedroom suite and here it was and I was alone. I went downstairs and slept on the couch.

The next morning, my brother Rick called and asked me about our plans for Christmas. Rick had recently moved out of my mother's house and into his girlfriend's place and was obviously thinking about the holidays. I told him we weren't doing anything and planned to celebrate quietly. Thinking about the holidays and my mother didn't even make it onto my radar. He suggested I invite Mom out for the holidays as she was feeling at a loss about what to do with herself. I said no, and brushed him off.

John and his brother Paul were planning a road trip to visit their younger brother Andrew in Ottawa who had just welcomed a baby boy into the world. John wanted to see the baby. I was angry that John's family didn't see what was happening and once again, I felt helpless and frustrated. The last thing John needed was to go travelling some more. He was unstable and delusional. Why could they not see it? John was not telling them everything and was hiding the worst of the delusions from his family.

That afternoon, they left Oakville and drove to Paul's house in Newcastle. They planned to stay the night at Paul's house and then head to Ottawa the next morning. I begged John's mom to stop them from going. I warned her it was dangerous and that John was unpredictable. Anything could happen. She said she needed time to think about what to do. She was not happy with me. I spoke to Paul on the phone one last time and told him I appreciated him wanting to help John but if he really wanted to help, he should have jumped on the airplane, come to Victoria and helped me get John into the frickin' hospital! That's it. I gave up. They could keep him!

Later that same night John sent me an unusual email. After twenty years, he wrote me a poem. Any other woman would be flattered. Once again, I was angry and stunned and wasn't sure what to make of it.

My Dear Mar,

The events of the day, week, and month have worn on me
On my heart and on my soul, and yours, yet you are there for me.
From the darkness of the valley of the shadow of death I still see
your light Gleaming,
at first weakly, star-like, but then with growing brilliance and
Beautiful rays of
Multicoloured effusion.
The warmth of your heart is my sun.
We converge and I am bathed in your wonderful glory
Transformed again after twenty-five years into a poet, I see the
world
In a better way, in a Regarding Henry wonder, but with the good
humour of Allan Ginsberg
Without the absurd offensiveness, you hate so much.
For you, I dreamt of love and mystical ascent of Mount Carmel.
You are not my god but a mirror of my soul, soul mate,
A human being, imperfect as me, yet I love you more for it.
You are a mirror of my soul, and I have dragged you down
through the depth of my
Darkest dreams. As I was looking at you, the mirror made me see
my own darkest
Dreams, not what you really are.
I see this clearly now and the mirror is finally recognized for
what it is.
And we pass through it, at last effortlessly, and into each other.
Now our love is

Transcendent, mystical, poetic and eternal.
Our two human souls are one. I am you and you are me. We are
one. We are only.
We are love, transcending all eternity.
Our eternal bliss and glory is knowing the perfect love for
another human being.
I love you my hon. I will always love you.
J*

He was reaching out to me in a way that only I would understand. I wasn't ready to buy into this. I wasn't ready to forgive and forget. Paul and his wife thought the poem was beautiful and didn't see what I saw. They told me not to talk to John's mom anymore because she was stressed out and looked terrible. If I needed someone to talk to, I should talk to one of them, not her. Peachy, I know.

I re-read the poem and tried to make sense of it. Was John offering me a glimmer of hope, an olive branch? Perhaps he wanted to show me that he was still there and he still loved me. How could I give up now? If I gave up on John now, would I be abandoning him? What do I do?

Chapter 12 - Morphed Like a Toy Transformer

The road trip to Ottawa went as planned. The three brothers, reunited, celebrated the new baby and spent the evening together as three brothers would after not seeing each other for a while. After all, these were far better circumstances than the last time they were together eight months before for their father's funeral. They sat around, reminisced and had a few drinks. John was able to keep it together for the most part while he was there and the visit took place incident free. He booked a flight to come home to Victoria the next day but not without Paul making me promise that I would allow him back in the house to spend Christmas at home with the kids. I made that promise but told Paul if John started making crazy accusations and questioning my fidelity and the paternity of the kids then he would have to leave again. I didn't care that it was Christmas.

I still had a day to myself and some time to think before John returned. I needed to come up with a plan. I wanted to find out what my options were and whom I could rely on for help. I was getting used to the idea that John was very ill and, even though we had no idea what exactly was wrong with him, I had to start considering that he might never be the same again. Was divorce really an option for us? I spent some time poking around on the internet trying to gather as much information I could about mental illnesses and possible side effects of *Abilify*. I started considering how I would look after myself, single, with three kids. I wondered what legal rights I had, and more importantly, what legal rights John had. Should I call our lawyer? Should I call the bank? It was all very overwhelming and I found that the internet could be a scary place. The kids were off school for the holidays and I was finding it difficult to be there for them and find time for myself. Sarah was amazing during this time and really was there for me. She showed moments of remarkable strength, responsibility and maturity. She was aware of what was happening and I kept her in the loop. I found it ironic that she wanted to go to university and study Psychiatry.

She stepped up to the plate and looked after her brothers when I needed her to and took them out when there was too much tension in the house. All the kids were sensitive to their dad's moodiness and feelings.

John and I are lucky to have such great kids and it made it easier for us deal with this difficult situation. In spite of everything, John is a good man. He is kind and generous and a good father. He is smart and works hard to provide for his family. He adores the kids and nothing matters to him more than his family.

I started to look back and recall specific events over the past few months and wonder how I didn't see this coming, or maybe I did and just didn't want to admit there might be something seriously wrong with my husband. For the first time I admitted that John had always been wary of people and often displayed paranoid traits. For example at a friend's wedding in July, John accused me of flirting and wanting to have sex with the bride's uncle because we were sitting and having a conversation about how he acquired an

NHL signet ring. He had an interesting life story and I am always curious and ask many questions. A few weeks later, I went out one evening to return something I had borrowed from a friend. We hadn't seen each other in a long time and we spent about an hour catching up with each other. When I returned home, John was furious with me. He wanted to know where I had been and what I had been doing. I explained but John was irrational and angry with me. He didn't want to believe two women, who hadn't seen each other in a while, would have no concept of time.

Sometime around the middle of August, John and I were out in our front yard doing some gardening, as was one of our neighbours. I crossed over the road and we were having a friendly conversation about plants and flowers. Not having the advantage of growing up in Victoria, gardening is a challenge for us and we were always thrilled whenever we successfully got anything to grow. We definitely had our share of failures with plants. This summer, I was proud of our garden and the neighbour was complimenting us on our efforts. John later accused me of throwing myself at him and was adamant that I ran across the street as soon as I saw him because I wanted to flirt with him.

In September, John noticed a tiny chip in his windshield. Convinced someone had pressed a staple gun into the glass, this upset him very much. He had been having a minor dispute at work over parking spaces and a neighbouring employee used a staple gun to hang a sign delineating the parking spaces in the lot. John also found a note on his car asking him to park tight to the right against the wall, allowing more room for the next car. Without any proof, John was convinced someone had vandalized his car.

He even went to the building security office to ask if surveillance cameras monitored that area. They didn't and this made John contemplate installing his own cameras. At the end of September, John became very angry with me for talking to the father of a boy that was dropping Sam off from a birthday party. I had learned during the day the little boy's grandfather had died that very morning and went out to offer my condolences. When I came back into the house, John accused me of being inappropriate and flirtatious and wanted to know what this man meant to me. Of course, there was the whole ferry incident that also happened in September, which I already mentioned. The illness was taking over and John was slipping away from me. September was such a bad month for us.

Now that I reflect back on these incidents, I can clearly see that John was not right. However, at the time these things were happening it just didn't occur to me something so terrible could be wrong. I remember thinking something was different about John but couldn't put my finger on it. My husband was slowly morphing, like a toy transformer, and we had no idea what was happening. I attributed his behaviour to work stress or being tired. I even tried to justify it sometimes as being cute or petty jealousy. I was reluctant to bring it up because it was not worth getting into yet another fight over it. Now we know these behaviours were warning symptoms or prodromal behaviour, but then we were not able to recognize them. Who would if they didn't already have some experience with mental illness?

Three days before Christmas, I picked John up from the Victoria Airport. He had lost more weight and looked pale but, thankfully, he didn't have crazy eyes. John told me he was feeling better and that while he was away he had gained some perspective and clarity. He told me the time he spent with his family made him realize how much he loved our family and he didn't feel those things anymore. He begged me for forgiveness and was genuinely remorseful and apologetic. He couldn't believe the things he had said to me and got embarrassed recalling the events. He regretted everything. He asked me to take him back and told me how much I meant to him and how much he loved me. We hugged and drove home.

When I asked John to go see Dr. G, he refused. I asked him if he at least would fill the prescription for the higher dosage of *Abilify* that the doctor had given me and he refused to do that also. He said he would wait until after the holidays and then he would go see Dr. G. I told John of my promise to his brother Paul and we called a truce for the sake of the kids, put on some brave faces and carried on.

Christmas happened quietly. I can't recall much about it and most of the holidays remain hazy for me. We kept to ourselves and didn't socialize the way we usually did except on New Year's. We received a last-minute invite from the parents of a little girl in Sam's class. I did not want to go. I was afraid to be around anyone and didn't want to give John an opportunity to accuse me of sleeping with someone. For some reason John insisted that we should go and I never figured out why it was so important to him. Perhaps he wanted to prove to me he could do it or maybe he thought *I* really wanted to go. Or maybe he was trying to make up for the past few months

It had been months since we had done anything or gone anywhere. I hadn't had any alcohol since John left the hospital and I was, if anything, looking forward to a drink.

John and I both drank It was a lovely party and we managed to get through the evening incident free although we definitely weren't our usual selves. If the host had known us a little better she would have recognized we were off our game. I was afraid to talk to the men for obvious reasons and John was friendly but quiet. I felt I had to stay by John's side the entire night. I just couldn't relax and be myself. I was expecting Delusional John to pop out any moment. Would this be my new life? Was this how it was going to be from now on? Would we ever be able to socialize like normal people? Would I ever enjoy another Ladies Night or be able to go shopping on my own without raising suspicion? I was a prisoner in my own home.

Chapter 13 - Release, Repair and Repaint

When the holidays were over and the kids had returned to school, I was looking to return to some sort of familiar routine. It was a new year after all and I wanted to be optimistic. What I really wanted was my old life back. I wanted my husband back. John went back to see Dr. G and agreed to start taking a higher dosage of *Abilify*. He was now at twenty-five milligrams and planned to go to thirty milligrams, the highest recommended dose, over the next two weeks. John was leery of the medication and suffering from some negative side effects of the medication. He could not sit still. He wanted to be moving all the time. He couldn't find a comfortable chair in the house. He would bounce from the couch to the chair and back again. His muscles ached. He would sit on the stairs, he would try lying in bed or on the floor, and he just couldn't relax. This is a condition called akathisia, one of the side effects of taking antipsychotic medication. The doctor prescribed another medication called *Clonazepam* to help John with this but it didn't seem to do much. I couldn't bear to see John so uncomfortable. My heart ached for him.

We went out a few times looking for new couch hoping John could get comfortable. We purchased a great couch but we had to wait over a month for delivery. The doctor also told us he hadn't had any luck in finding a psychiatrist willing to take on John's case. How could that be? Why wouldn't they see him? It turns out that getting in to see a psychiatrist in this province is very difficult. The system is already overloaded with too many patients requiring on-going care. There simply isn't room for new patients. The best place to see a psychiatrist during an emergency is probably in the hospital.

Dr. G referred John's case to four psychiatrists and each psychiatrist rejected it. Nonetheless, we asked the doctor to keep pursuing a psychiatrist. We trusted Dr. G and felt confident he was treating John effectively but he was a GP and not a psychiatrist. We wanted John to see a psychiatrist who had more experience in the mental health area. We didn't think this was too much to ask.

One night just after getting into bed, I opened a jar of body cream John had given me as a Christmas gift. I used some on my hands and a moment later reached over and touched John's shoulder. He startled me as he smacked my hand away. "Don't touch me with those creamy hands!"

"What's wrong?"

"You don't know what's in that stuff!"

"It's only body lotion. You bought it for me! Do you want me to read you a list of the ingredients?"

Delusional John was always lurking about. I decided to let it go because no matter what I said he was going to think bad things about me. I turned out the lamp, rolled over and cried myself to sleep while he lay awake thinking I was going to poison him by way of body lotion.

John was still not back at work and the plan was for him to return to work part-time in February. I still wasn't working in any sort of a meaningful capacity but was only managing to answer my phone and e-mails. Howie and Maria continued to cover for me and kept our secret while we were trying to get John stabilized and feeling better. We seldom heard from his family and I wondered if they thought he was better or maybe they just assumed all was well if they didn't hear from us. We spent almost all of our time together. I was afraid to go anywhere by myself. If John wasn't with me I would take one of the kids as an alibi. We did the grocery shopping together as well as the school pick-ups and drop-offs and any errands we had.

One shopping trip got particularly exciting when the cashier and I engaged in a conversation about eggplants. She had never tasted one and I suggested she get someone to cook it for her who knows what they're doing. John got it into his head that I had been meeting with a secret lover who liked to cook eggplant for me. We started fighting in the car on the way home, by the time we came into the house we were in full combat mode, and I was staring at crazy eyes again.

"Just admit it! You have been meeting someone who cooks for you haven't you?"

"No! No I haven't."

"Well I know you have. I just know it." "Just tell me the truth I can take it."

"There is nothing to tell. I haven't done anything," I screamed back and then something suddenly occurred to me. I realized that whenever I looked into his eyes the bad thoughts about me were always going to be there. It's as if the delusions had become ingrained in his brain like a bad habit that keeps repeating over and over again. I looked at John and felt the loss. I tasted defeat. I knew at that moment

119

it was over for us. Our bond was broken and he was not in love with me anymore. I simply couldn't bear it. Then something strong and powerful welled up inside of me and I let loose.

"You are flippin' crazy!" I yelled as loud as I could. "Look what you are doing! Can't you see what is going on here?" Then before I could stop it, something else happened. I lost control as I was yelling at John and I peed myself. I couldn't believe it. I freakin' wet my pants! I was mortified, humiliated and shocked. I ran upstairs to the bedroom and locked the door. I fell to my knees and started bawling. Then I got angry. Not the kind of anger when someone dings your car door or when one of the kids breaks something good in the house, but really deep, dark anger.

This anger came from some place I didn't know existed inside of me. I stood up and started throwing things. I threw our radio that sat on my dresser. I threw shoes, a jar of salt scrub and books. I threw anything I could get my hands on. It felt so good to release that pent-up anger and frustration. John's laptop was on the bed and I picked it up and tucked it under my arm, not sure what I intended to do with it. I threw more things: a bunch of hangers, a wooden trinket box, body lotion. I picked up things that I had already thrown once and threw them again. Several holes appeared in the dry wall and I didn't care. This felt good. I was enjoying the release. I just wanted to feel something. Anything was better than the pain and hurt I was suffering at that moment. I had gone from loving this man with all my heart to hating him in the matter of minutes. John knocked on the door, asked me what I was doing and yelled at me to stop it. I ignored him and threw a shoe at the wall. He yelled again for me to stop throwing things and tried to come in but I had locked the door. I flung two books at once towards the door and screamed, "Go away!"

"Mar, please open the door." He pleaded once more. John could easily have broken through the door with sheer force but for some reason decided not to and left me to my business.

Then without thinking, the laptop still in my left hand I hurled it right at the door. *Holy shit!* I had totally lost it! I was so mad he was interrupting my release. This was *my* moment and I wanted it to myself. How dare he try to stop me? He got all the doctors, the psychiatrists and the drugs, and all I got was abuse, accusations and pee-pee pants. I felt weak in the knees after my tirade and collapsed on the floor, inhaling and exhaling huge breaths of air nearing the point of hyperventilating.

I shut my eyes tight, willing everything to slow down and stop spinning. My thoughts were all over the place. Snapshots of our life together flashed through my mind like a slideshow. Our teenage years. Our babies. Christmas mornings. Camping trips. Lazy Saturdays. Cocktail parties. Picnics. Moving vans. Birthdays. What had happened to our beautiful happy life? Could it really be over for us? I continued to lie on the floor with my eyes closed waiting for my breathing to return to normal.

I came out of the bedroom a little while later, in a clean set of clothes feeling somewhat refreshed. I just wasn't sure if our love was strong enough to keep us together. I probably believed it wasn't. I had always believed there was nothing in this entire world that would separate us. We loved each other too much and naively I believed we would always be together. We sat down and talked. John apologized and told me he didn't think that I had a secret-chef-lover-boyfriend anymore, but I knew he still thought it. I think he was afraid that next time I would be hurling objects at his head. I was getting better at this. We talked some more and both agreed he needed to be on a higher dose of medication. The problem was the side effects of the *Abilify* were beyond what John could tolerate. Even after a long walk John was restless and his muscles coiled up and were jittery.

His next appointment wasn't for two weeks and John decided to ride it out hoping that perhaps the side effects would subside. He was due to return to work and hoping that once he was back at work the akathisia would settle down. He also wanted to wait to see a psychiatrist before starting the highest recommended dose of *Abilify* when it didn't seem to be working anyway. John's psychologist, Bob, called from time to time to get an update about John and seemed sincerely concerned and still perplexed as to what was wrong with John. If he did know, he certainly wasn't saying.

I told him about my rant in the bedroom and received a modest absolution from him, even though I was not distressed about it in the slightest. I never would have thrown anything about if the kids had been around and I don't plan to do something like that ever again. Fortunately the laptop survived.

John was great about repairing the holes I had made in the drywall and on the back of the bedroom door and re-painted. Incidentally, John was worried about me and felt I needed someone to talk to. He suggested I find a therapist of my own and seek counselling. I wondered if it wasn't a divorce attorney I should be seeking. I knew very little about counselling and did a quick search on the internet. I picked the first one I could find closest to our home and made an appointment for two days later.

I found the session somewhat helpful but also recognized that no one was going to help us through this. We would have to manage the cards we were dealt in a health care system that was slow to react and ineffectual for our purposes. I was beginning to feel like we were stuck in a living nightmare and couldn't get out. I tried not to feel sorry for myself and needed to be strong for John and especially the children. He needed me more now than ever and I couldn't fall apart. Not now. This is one test I was determined to pass.

There seemed to be a never-ending number of phone calls and extensive paper work needing to be filled-out for John's health care coverage. We had to work with a care manager from OHI, a private health insurance company that his organization contracted to manage short-term disability.

On one of OHI's forms, John checked off a box indicating he was interested in a referral to a specialist. We were told that it might take a month or longer to arrange something with a specialist because extra funds needed to be secured and signatures were required. We were thrilled when John got an appointment after waiting one long month from the time of submitting the forms. John was finally going to get the chance to see a psychiatrist and we were really looking forward to this appointment and getting some answers.

As it turned out, the appointment was more for OHI than it was for John. Dr. M, the psychiatrist, told John that he would not be discussing his condition with him but rather he would provide a written report to OHI. Dr. M asked John to sign a document agreeing to the disclosure before the session even started. John recognized what was happening and it came as a huge blow to him. He couldn't have been more disappointed. John told Dr. M his story and answered all his questions, which felt more like an interrogation for John.

Fifty-five minutes later, John was on his way home feeling duped and realizing that OHI had wanted proof of John's illness, independent of the family doctor. Here we were looking for help and no diagnosis was given or even discussed. When John returned from the appointment and told me what happened, I was furious. He called his healthcare manager and conveniently her voicemail picked-up. The next day after John spoke with the manager and told her how disappointed he was with this appointment and how he felt duped, he learned that a copy of Dr. M's report would be sent to the family doctor. John asked for a copy to be sent to him also but was told he would have to obtain it from the family doctor. This is what the diagnosis says:

Mr. Gibson presents with severe anxiety associated with profound disorder of judgement. He appears to have persisting beliefs of his wife's infidelity. Mr. Gibson's beliefs in October were considerably more bizarre. I would not see this as being a circumscribed and simple delusional disorder. On the other hand, it is not simply a brief reactive psychosis because of the persistence of symptoms. It is not sufficient at this time to make a diagnosis of schizophrenia. There does not appear to be clear enough evidence of the symptomology being precipitated by alcohol use. I would not make any diagnosis of alcohol abuse or dependence based upon the history.

There was no discussion of John's medication or the dosages. There was no discussion, period. Right around the same time, Dr. G managed to get a one-time appointment for John with a different psychiatrist, one that was willing to talk directly to John about his condition. Unfortunately, this appointment was more of a disaster than the one with the first psychiatrist.

Dr. N was a very old doctor who seemed to be living in his own delusional state. When John spoke of his wife's infidelity, the doctor encouraged him to hire a private investigator to see what his wife was really doing. He suggested surprise pop in visits at home to catch me in the act or perhaps have his friends drop in on me. In essence, he was proposing that John do whatever he needed to, to determine what I was really doing. Dr. N reminded John that similar stories of infidelity go far back in time and play out much like a Shakespearean drama. He didn't have any real diagnosis for John and didn't think much was wrong with him.

Again, there was no discussion about John's medication and whether or not it was working or if it was even the right type of medication for him. When John returned and told me what the doctor had said, I was speechless. Thankfully, John recognized the flaw in the doctor's recommendation, didn't see much value in the advice, and dismissed it as worthless. However, John optimistically tried to extract something positive from this appointment and believed that if he was going to get better, he'd have to prove to himself I wasn't doing anything and just get over it already.

Chapter 14 - Back in the Hospital

February arrived and John returned to work half days after being off for three months. He was nervous and worried about what people would say to him. He was especially worried someone would ask why he was away or what was wrong with him. The only thing I could do was assure him that polite people don't ask such questions and he isn't obligated to answer. People should know better.

It felt good to have John out of the house and away from me for part of the day. I finally could have some time to myself and I tried to get back to work myself in a more productive capacity. Howie and Maria continued to be there for me and I kept them informed of John's progress, which really couldn't be described as progress at all. I knew John was still having some delusions but rarely talked about them anymore. I could see the look in his eyes and how tormented he was. We were all hopeful for John and to see him want to get back to work was a good thing.

Every morning after John left for work and the kids went to school, I would sit at my computer and try to work. Many days I just sat there staring at my computer screen paralysed by an emotion I can only describe as grief. I had learned enough by now about delusional disorders and mental illnesses to know that I would never have my husband back the way he once was. He was a changed man. He was not the man I fell in love with twenty-six years ago. When I thought about all the horrible things he had said to me and the look on his face while saying it, I wondered how we could ever salvage something good from this. Was there any hope for us? Would the hurt eventually fade away? We were once happy and now we were sad.

I read about suicide statistics and learned it is higher for people with mental illnesses and the same for divorce rates. Would we fall into these stats? No matter which way I looked at it, the future looked grim. I was losing my optimism and felt cheated, and that made me angry. I hated John for what he had done to our happy family. I couldn't do my work and that made me angry. Several times, while speaking with Maria, I told her I wanted to quit working. I just wasn't able to function. The kids needed me, and John needed me, and I didn't know if there was enough of me to go around. Then again my income was needed and John didn't need the added stress of worrying about our finances.

John was obsessing about money and worried about our financial future. This was not the time for me to quit my job. John was going to work for four hours a day and we would spend the rest of the time together talking and trying to rebuild our relationship. Before John's illness emerged in October, we had booked a family vacation to Costa Rica for early April and we didn't know whether John would be well enough to travel or if it was even a good idea to leave the country. John was still not stable and was suffering from the akathisia worse than ever. He would spend much of his time pacing from one end of the room to the other and still could not relax unless he was asleep.

We kept in touch with John's mother and sometimes she would ask about John and sometimes she wouldn't. I think mental illness is so hard to comprehend and accept that people tend to avoid talking about it at all. If this could happen to someone like John, then it's possible that it could happen to anyone. I suppose we all handle difficult situations differently.

I tried to talk to my own mother about once a week to keep her off our trail. The last thing I needed was for her to get suspicious that something was wrong. One evening, Mom and I had an awful argument about something work related. When you work with family though, work-related problems become personal problems and it is difficult if not impossible to separate the two. I felt terribly distraught about the situation. I did tell her we were going to Costa Rica for a holiday.

By the end of February, John became delusional again. This episode was worse than anything he had experienced before. One morning, John woke me up at five o'clock.

"Mar? Can you get up? I am not feeling well and we need to talk."

"What's wrong?"

"Please, can you just get up and come downstairs?"

I joined John down in the living room and asked him what was wrong? He wouldn't sit down and was pacing back and forth. He told me he was thinking terrible things and he didn't want to believe that they were true but he couldn't make his mind stop. He was almost frantic and when I saw his crazy eyes were back, I got scared. "Let's go for a walk." I suggested. Instinctively we headed out on our usual walking route circling the neighbourhood. We walked every day and John was steadily losing weight. Once out in the fresh air, I was hoping John would gain some clarity.

"Do you want to tell me what's going on?"

"No I can't. It's too bad. It's really, really bad and trust me, you don't want to know."

We continued walking and John tried to talk about other things but couldn't put two thoughts together in any sensible manner. He was just too distracted.

"Did you even sleep last night? How long have you been awake?" I asked.

"I slept a little. Not much. It's the medication. It's not working. I feel terrible."

"Well we should go back to the doctor right away." "It's Saturday and I can't wait until Monday."

"Okay, well why don't you tell me what the bad thoughts are and then we can figure out what to do?

"I told you I don't want to tell you."

"I know! But if you don't tell me, how can I help you?"

"Okay, this is what I am thinking…"

What John had to say was mortifying not only to me, but also to him. Our son Daniel had brought a few friends home after school the day before to work on a school project. They needed to film a scene from Romeo and Juliette and wanted to work downstairs in our family room. While they were getting set-up, Daniel asked me to help him find costumes and props. I went downstairs and into the crawlspace to find what they needed. I left John sitting in our living room. It took me about fifteen minutes and I managed to find everything they needed. Mission accomplished.

John thought that while I was down in the crawlspace supposedly finding costumes, I was doing "things" with the teenage boys. This was disturbing to both of us because it was so opposite to John's kind and gentle nature. In fact, all the thoughts of infidelity and talk about my histrionic personality and flirtatious behaviour were anything but what the real John was like. John was not a crude or vulgar person. He was very respectful and thoughtful. He didn't swear, spit or use curse words around the children or me. That kind of behaviour I was used to from my two older brothers, but not John. This just was so unlike John and this time I knew we needed to do something drastic. Before this day, the delusions were mostly about me. Now the delusions incorporated the children and this worried me.

"Okay that's just sick." I spat out in disgust. "You have reached an all-time low. What you are thinking is awful! It's gross! Criminal! How could you think I could do such a thing?" I felt nauseous.

"I know it's bad. I am sick. I need help. I don't believe it really. I just can't stop thinking it, that's all." Nevertheless, inside I knew he had doubts and could not separate reality from the delusions. He was trying to be brave but was completely confused.

We walked in silence for a while so I could cool down and regain some of my composure. I needed to absorb what was happening. All I could think was, here we go again. I wanted off this rollercoaster. I was shocked at what John had just confessed to me and didn't know how to deal with it. I wanted to suggest he needed to be back in the hospital right away but was afraid to mention it. It was raining and surprisingly warm for February as we started our second lap around the neighbourhood. It was still dark and I could smell the ocean and faintly hear a foghorn blowing in the distance.

Even though we were both raised going to church, neither of us are religious, except the time back in December when John found Jesus. But at this moment I seriously contemplated a prayer or two. I didn't feel the need to pray out of desperation but rather considered whether it would be worthwhile. After all, John was sick and the things he said and thought were not his fault.

Inside I knew John was a good person. He didn't really need prayers to get better rather he needed better medication and time for it to work. I didn't want to pray for myself because that seemed rather self-absorbed and egocentric. I wasn't really into asking for anything from the higher powers. I needed strength and I believe that comes from within.

So what did I want at that moment? Granted one wish, what would it be? I just wanted it to stop. Stop the accusations, stop the delusions, stop the hurt, stop crying, stop yelling, stop the medication and stop the doctor's appointments. I wanted it all to stop and have my life back even if it was just for a day. I love John so much but was love enough to fight this? I always wanted to believe love would conquer all but now I wasn't so sure.

Basically, we had two options at this point. We could take John back to the emergency psychiatric facility at the hospital or call the emergency crisis team that makes house calls. We debated which option would be best and John surprised me by choosing to go to the hospital. All

John could think about was getting off the *Abilify* and hopefully onto some other kind of medication and he needed a psychiatrist to do that. Driving to the hospital, I asked John several times if he was sure that this is what he wanted and each time he said it was. Just before we reached the hospital entrance, John bailed and changed his mind. "I can't do it. I hate this place." I drove past the entrance and around the block. "Never mind, we can go home and call the Crisis team."

"No. I should do this."

"So you want to go in?"

"No. I can't."

"John, if you want to go in, I'll stay with you. I promise I won't leave you. We will do this together. I promise I won't leave."

"Do you think I can just talk to a psychiatrist and get a new prescription? That's all I need. I'll take anything else but this stuff. It's awful!"

"I don't know, but we will never know if we don't go in there and ask."

John took a deep breath, looked at me with his crazy eyes and said, "Okay, let's do this."

We went through the check-in process and found ourselves sitting at a small round table at the end of the room. Everything looked the same and I don't know why but I expected to see the same patients in the room. It was still early in the morning and there were only about half the number of people as when we were there last. We waited for about an hour and then a young woman came over, introduced herself, explained that she was a psychiatric intern and invited John into a meeting room to talk.

After twenty minutes, John came back and joined me at our table. The Intern left to speak with the on-call doctor and said she would get back to John. We had no idea how long this process was going to take and the only thing we could do was to sit and wait. Some of the patients were up and aimlessly moving about while others lay on the recliners, blue shrouds covering them from head to toe while their breakfast trays sat cold and untouched.

It didn't take long before the young intern came over to our table and invited both of us into a meeting room. Another female doctor joined us. I recognized her from John's initial hospital stay. The on-call psych doctor was a very short woman who didn't sit down while speaking with us. She was almost eye level with John's six foot two stature while he was sitting. The first thing she explained was that until they sorted out John's medication he was being put on a forty-eight hour mandatory hold in the hospital. She explained that whenever someone shows a break from reality, in essence psychosis, that as the physician she is obligated to protect not only the ill person but also society in general.

Wow! This was disappointing for John but he took the news like a trooper and handled it well. He looked at me with such pain and anguish on his face that it broke my heart. I felt like crying but my tears had dried up weeks ago.

The rest of the conversation was about discussing a plan to switch out John's meds and give him something to manage the withdrawal symptoms. I lost track of the conversation for a brief moment and my thoughts wandered to worrying about Delusional John thinking I had something to do with him being locked up in the hospital again. I felt badly because I had to break my promise to him that I wasn't going to leave him. This wasn't my fault. I didn't know this would happen. The two doctors agreed that the current medication wasn't effectively treating his illness and a change was warranted.

I took this opportunity to ask exactly what illness they were treating John for because after four months of delusions, some serious antipsychotic medication, two independent psychiatry consults, not including the three psychiatrists he spoke with the first time in hospital, we still didn't know what was wrong with John! Still standing, the on-call doctor flipped through the file and called John's illness Delusional Disorder NOS. The NOS part means Not Otherwise Specified. They didn't have enough information to diagnose him any further.

I later learned that it takes months and months to diagnose someone with a particular mental disorder and, even then, it is highly speculative. It isn't as if there were a blood test or brain scan that proves a diagnosis. The doctors wanted to consult with another psychiatrist and ushered us back into the lounge area. Now we had nothing to do but sit and wait. The waiting was really getting to me and I became impatient and restless. The last thing John needed was for me to get him worked up about all the waiting around. I asked him if he would be all right alone for a while and offered to go get him some extra clothes and some toiletries. At the same time I was hesitant to leave because I didn't want to miss John's next appointment with the psychiatrists—no time was given.

There were other times when we were left to wait without being given any indication of how long the wait would be or what we were waiting for.

I left the hospital and made it back in time to meet with a new psychiatrist who had a plan for John's medication. The plan weaned John off *Abilify* over the next seven days. The new antipsychotic drug they prescribed was *Risperidone,* two milligrams. They also prescribed two milligrams of *Benztropine* to be taken for five days—it is commonly used for Parkinson's patients to help with the shakes—and seven and a half milligrams of *Zopiclone,* a mild sedative. We were not familiar with any of these medications and could barely even pronounce them.

Prior to John's illness, our medicine box had consisted of *Advil, Band-Aids,* expired cough syrup and an assortment of heartburn medications. Before we left the hospital this time, I made sure to ask for follow-up psychiatric care. I learned from our last experience that as long as John had a loving wife at home and a warm bed to sleep in every night, the health care system was all too happy to send him home expecting the family doctor to provide on-going care. This didn't seem right. The family doctor was doing his best but he was not a specialist. John needed a psychiatrist and needed one who was willing to spend more than one hour with him. Even though it was a long shot, I insisted that John be recommended for follow-up care with a psychiatrist before we left the hospital. John was so relieved to be off the *Abilify* he was happy to take the new drugs.

The nurses were a little more relaxed with John this time and allowed us to leave the locked area and walk about the hospital. We went and bought some tea and found a quiet area where we could sit and talk. John was feeling a little better knowing that he was going to get off the Abilify but I sensed that something was still troubling him. I started asking questions to find out what it was. After a while, John told me that he suspected I was pregnant again. Sharp pains squeezed my heart and I suddenly realized John was still delusional. He told me he didn't think it was our baby and that I was acting as a surrogate for another couple who couldn't have a baby. I don't know why he would think that but then there was no sense to the delusions, a lesson I was slowly learning. I didn't take it personally and managed to stay calm and not fight with him. He was going to have to stay in the hospital for a couple more days and I didn't want to make it any harder on him than it was already going to be.

I received a phone call on my cell phone and learned the nurses were getting a little nervous about where we were. They explained that the breaks were meant to be only fifteen minutes. I walked John back to the entrance of the emergency psychiatric area. We hugged each other and he gave me a kiss goodnight. A kiss I cherished.

It was too late to call John's mom by the time I returned home and I really didn't feel like talking to anyone. I just wanted to be with my kids. Sarah made me a cup of tea and we sat in the living room and talked while the boys played computer games downstairs. Sarah wanted to know all the details and asked many questions. I answered them as honestly as I could and didn't hide anything from her.

Sunday morning, I got up early and brought breakfast to the hospital for John. Considering what had happened the last time he was in the hospital, I wasn't sure if he was going to eat or drink anything at all. I didn't know what to expect. Thankfully, he drank the tea, but said he had been up early himself and had eaten his breakfast already and was happy to keep the egg sandwich for later. I was suspicious but decided to let it go. What was the point of arguing with a "crazy" man in the psych ward? He was there to get help and this was the best place for him to find it. Did it really matter if he wasn't going to eat?

After the forty-eight hour waiting period concluded, John was allowed to leave the hospital and remarkably returned to work full-time the next day on the first of March. This may have been over zealous on his part but he just wanted to get back to work and to normal life again. John started to feel better almost immediately, and he improved daily until the end of March when he was feeling significantly better and the akathisia had disappeared.

John travelled for the first time in months and went away for two days on a business trip. I was extremely worried that something might happen while he was gone. Everything went great during the trip except for feeling a little rusty on presentation skills. The akathisia was a bad memory and John was sleeping almost ten hours a night. With the new medication came a new hope and we felt optimistic that John was going to recover and we could finally move on with our lives.

Chapter 15 - Renewal

On the first day of April, the atmosphere in the house was the happiest it had been in months. The kids could sense John's mood had lightened and pranked him several times for April Fools' Day. They booby-trapped the kitchen faucet so John would get sprayed with water when he turned it on and they also left a very convincing rubber rat on the front step for him to stumble upon. Traditionally, the kids and I pranked John unmercifully every April Fools' Day with the exception of one year when we didn't do anything at all. John was on edge the entire day waiting for something to scare him, and when nothing materialized, he realized that was the premise of our joke.

Everyone was looking forward to our trip to Costa Rica. John and I were especially excited because we had decided to go through with our original plan to renew our marriage vows while we were there. Neither of us was prepared to voice our concerns and we counted on good things happening. It was our twentieth wedding anniversary on the twenty-first of March and with everything going on with John, it seemed perfect to celebrate this anniversary in a big way. We needed something good to happen in our lives.

Our high school friend Tim had moved to Costa Rica seventeen years previously and lives there with his wife, Marjorie and their fifteen year-old son. We were looking forward to spending time with all of them. Kindly, Marjorie arranged the vow renewal ceremony and dinner. All we had to do was show up. Although I still trod on eggshells around John, the new medication seemed to be working and the delusions were slowly leaving John alone. Before we left, there was one more psychiatric appointment for John, arranged by the hospital psychiatrists as a follow up to his last admission.

Coincidentally, it was with the same psychiatrist that OHI had used for their fake appointment/inquisition. Awkward as it was, John and the doctor handled themselves professionally and spent an hour discussing John's illness after which the doctor provided John with a new diagnosis. Dr. M told John he didn't think it was quite a delusional disorder but something similar because the nature of the delusions was bizarre but had not ingrained firm beliefs. John did not exactly fit the criteria for the more common mental illnesses and, without more time, a comprehensive diagnosis was very difficult. John returned home and we discussed the mediocrity of the appointment and decided to put it aside. Our attention turned to our trip and there was laundry and packing to do. We had more important things to think about like sunshine and hot weather.

Our trip to Costa Rica was wonderful and everybody had a great time. We were happy to visit with our friends Tim and Marjorie who were gracious and hospitable hosts. After a day to relax by their swimming pool, we visited a wildlife zoo, went to an active volcano, zip-lined eleven runs totalling over ten kilometres, went horseback riding, fed wild crocodiles and went to the beach. The kids loved the beach and couldn't get enough time in the water.

One afternoon John was jumping in the waves with the kids as I sat on the beach and watched them. I watched my precious family laughing and screaming with excitement as each surge swallowed them under the surface of the water and tumbled them onto the beach like discarded sea debris. With the heat of the sun on my body and the turquoise-coloured ocean in front of me, I momentarily forgot about John's illness and the delusions and the accusations and the crazy eyes of the past several months. I was happy for a few minutes, I think, but then thoughts of my brutal reality returned and sank my heart like feet partially buried and stuck in wet sand.

My highlight of the trip was definitely our vow renewal ceremony. Marjorie had organized the event at an amazing little boutique hotel with a Greek theme, located high up in the mountains overlooking the ocean. We spent the day in our rented suite and lounged around in our own hot tub on our private balcony. We had an amazing view of the jungle and could hear all the exotic animals. Sarah arrived early to help me get dressed and do my hair for the ceremony. My best friend and one of my original bridesmaids, Joanne flew in from Atlanta with her new baby to join us. I was supposed to fly down to be with her for the birth in January but with John as sick as he was, that obviously didn't happen. I was so happy she was there and I had a chance to meet the baby. I had told Joanne about John's illness only a few weeks before our trip and she now understood why I couldn't be there for her when she was having the baby.

We exchanged our vows in front of our closest friends and children on a covered patio, high up on a hillside at sunset. The weather was perfect and the setting

141

was very romantic. We sat at a big table and had dinner together, cut a beautiful little wedding cake and danced to Rod Stewart's, *You're in my Heart*. It was a wonderful event for us and I will always cherish this moment. Whatever happens to us in the future, wherever this horrible, evil disease takes us, we both knew at that moment on that day, how much we loved each other.

April 2012. Costa Rica. Vow renewal.

The rest of April found John experiencing new side effects and unwanted symptoms from the *Risperidone*. He was feeling down and melancholy. He was getting anxious about work and worried about contracts and loss of business. He wasn't eating very much and had to poke a new hole in his belt and buy new pants. He had lost almost sixty pounds. He was losing interest in the kids and in me. Sex was no longer happening and seemed unimportant to him. We rarely talked intimately or about anything meaningful and spending time together felt like a burden for me.

It was painful to take a walk together and not have a significant thing to say to each other. I was afraid to say anything to John about how I was feeling for fear of triggering an episode or risking him feeling guilty for his illness. John's recovery remained the focus of my attention but I truly missed being happy. I was desperately homesick in my own home and in my own bed. We were becoming strangers to each other.

These issues continued into May and John lacked motivation to work at his job. I noticed him changing and he seemed depressed much of the time. He seemed flat and bored and then would suddenly flip to being anxious and fixated on certain ideas. He was disorganized and found it difficult to concentrate on anything for more than a few minutes. He was frustrated that he couldn't do what he once did. It saddened me to see what was happening to my husband. I was losing hope that he would return to the strong, independent and proud man that he once was.

John became self-conscious and timid and didn't want to socialize at all. It had been months since we had gone anywhere or entertained at our home, something we used to love to do. He was no longer confident and he worried about his job constantly. He had periodic feelings of hopelessness and despair. I felt helpless not knowing how to help my husband. His depression became contagious and I began to feel miserable again also. We rarely joked and smiling was rare.

John had to travel to Calgary for work and was going to be gone three days. I was worried that being away from me would trigger an episode and feared the worst could happen. I didn't want John to lose it in front of his colleagues, which could potentially ruin his career. I was also secretly glad John was gone for a few days and this made me feel guilty. I was exhausted and emotionally drained from all the drama. I knew a few days apart from John would give me a rest and some renewed energy to face the next round of delusions whenever that might be. I rarely slept through the night waking up every hour or two, or I would end up staying awake for hours contemplating our future. I was always on the lookout for Delusional John watching John closely, monitoring his behaviour, trying to predict his moods.

With John out of the house and the kids at school all day, I returned to the internet and started poking around, researching different mental illnesses, unsatisfied with the lack of diagnoses or the lose diagnoses we received without any prognosis. This made both of us unsettled and uncomfortable, and I wanted answers!

On the computer I creeped psychiatry forums, discussion boards and personal blogs on the internet. I read articles published in psychiatric journals and tried to learn as much as I could about mental illnesses and paranoid behaviour. I read articles about delusional disorders and jealousy and persecutory beliefs. I cross-matched John's original symptoms in search engines hoping to get hits on more research papers. I went to bookstores and then the library, and it was at the library that I started getting answers. I borrowed five books on mental illness, two of which were about schizophrenia. I started reading one particular book in the parking lot of the library and before I knew it, I had sat there for three hours devouring the information I was reading. The more I read about schizophrenia, the more I recognized my husband. Over the next couple of days, I read several memoirs written by people suffering from schizophrenia and deep in my heart I believed that this was what John was suffering from.

******

John

I travelled to Calgary on a business trip, which was my first trip away from home alone in a long time. I was tired of taking my meds, suffering from a bit of depression, and most of all I was curious to see whether I would feel better without them. So I took advantage of the opportunity away and skipped taking my Risperidone for three days. I felt like colours were more vivid and sounds were more crisp, but I also decided that perhaps it was too risky, that I might lose my equilibrium if I kept it up. I took my meds again on day four. I am still curious what might have happened if I had stayed off them for longer.

******

Luckily, John returned home from Calgary incident free and told me about his medicine infraction. I hoped that the *Risperidone* was working better than the *Abilify*. I could only go by what John was telling me about what was happening in his head. I had no way to tell and had to wait it out. If he said he was fine, I had to believe he was fine. It was hard for me to trust him, as I am sure it was hard for him to trust me. What I did know was that John was sleeping soundly nine to ten hours a night and he had lost the crazy eyes. He hadn't had a delusion for quite a while or at least he didn't talk about it if he did. The more I learned about schizophrenia and the more I thought about John's symptoms, I couldn't help but wonder why the family doctor and all the psychiatrists evaded what seemed like an

145

obvious diagnosis to me now. What did I know that the doctors didn't?

Chapter 16 - Accepting Schizophrenia

I was anxious to tell John that I had been researching different mental illnesses and that I had some ideas about what was happening with him. I wasn't sure how he was going to perceive what I had to say and didn't want to upset him. I was nervous that he would be angry, and I was terrified of triggering another psychotic event. John knew I would do anything for him and that meant help his recovery also. I decided just to come out with it as he was in no position to be angry with me for anything at this point. We were both trying really hard to get over the events of the past few months. I asked him to read one particular book, a memoir actually, about schizophrenia and he willingly agreed.

John immediately recognized the similarities of his own symptoms with those of the author's. He made the connection and could easily relate what happened to the author with what happened to him. The delusions, the psychosis, the paranoia, it was all unnervingly similar. After finishing the book, John finally admitted that what he was experiencing were real delusions and confessed that he had been trying to deny it up until now. He also admitted that what happened seven years ago when he suspected me of having an affair with his co-worker was because of similar paranoid delusions. He recognized all the events in the summer and fall as prodromal behaviour, which preceded the nasty psychotic break in October. He agreed with my suspicions and considered his condition might very well be schizophrenia.

John was anxious to see Dr. G the next day to discuss the depressive side effects he was experiencing and talk to him about what we suspected. He also wanted to discuss either lowering the *Risperidone* to eliminate the depression or maybe try a different antipsychotic drug. John also was ready to talk to the doctor about the many delusions he had experienced over the past several months that he had previously kept mum about. We were hoping what John had to say would help Dr. G. put a few more pieces of the puzzle into place and bring us closer to a more accurate diagnosis. We wanted to hear what the doctor thought. This was a very important step for John, admitting that indeed he had been suffering from delusions all along and actually understanding what a delusion essentially is. John finally accepted that he was suffering from mental illness and was ready to face it head-on.

How do we do all this in a ten-minute appointment? We made a list. John told the doctor that he was feeling depressed and asked if these were side effects of the *Risperidone*. The doctor was leaning more towards the idea that the *Risperidone* dosage was too low and these symptoms of disorganization, despair, anguish and depression would go away with an increased dose. John also revealed the extent of his delusions and talked about what happened seven years ago.

When we asked about a diagnosis, the doctor was still hesitant about labelling John with a particular illness. He wasn't sure if John's illness was in the schizophrenic category. I don't know why it seemed so important to us after waiting all these months. Maybe it was because we were tired of waiting. Anyone who has ever waited for a biopsy result or the results of a blood test knows what waiting to hear about your health does to a person. It fundamentally puts your life on hold. There is no moving forward, no plans can be made, nothing gets accomplished. Waiting is hell.

John went on to mention that he had experienced similar delusions in his twenties. When we brought our new baby home from the hospital, John spent a week or so believing that my mother had killed our two cats fearing they might harm Sarah. The cats actually did disappear for a couple of days but that is not unusual behaviour for fastidious little felines. They can get very skittish when something changes in the house. John searched the bushes around our house, checked the garbage bins and opened garbage bags. He even climbed up on the roof looking for them, and all the while, they just decided to go camping for a few days while everything settled down in the house.

Knowing that mental illness can run in families, John felt compelled to tell the doctor about a relative displaying similar bizarre and paranoid behaviour. Dr. G recorded more notes in the file and said he wanted to consult with the last psychiatrist John had visited and determine if any additional medication was necessary or a change in the dosage of the antipsychotic drug was warranted. By the end of this appointment, the doctor said that John was definitely suffering from a form of schizophrenia. We left with the impression that the doctor wasn't committed to that diagnosis and there was the possibility that there may be more than one illness.

John was brave to be forthright with the doctor and willingly able to discuss the paranoia and delusions openly and honestly. I was proud of him. Admitting that he had suffered from delusions in the past was a very difficult thing for him to do. Knowing there is something wrong with your brain is freakishly scary. Talking about it is scarier. This huge step aided John's recovery process. John met with the doctor a couple of days later and he prescribed *Cipralex*, to help with the depression, and left the *Risperidone* dosage where it was. It was doing its job by keeping the delusions away.

John and I decided it was time to tell my mother about John's illness. She was initially shocked by the news as I expected her to be. I had asked Maria to sit with her while I told her because I didn't want her to be alone. I talked to my mother several times during the next couple of days because she needed time to absorb everything I was telling her and, like everyone else, she knew very little about schizophrenia or any other mental illness. She made a few offensive remarks and asked some insensitive questions, but I do not blame her for that. She was in shock and denial herself, a natural response to such horrific news. She decided to start reading about the illness and did a fair amount of her own research and I appreciate her willingness to learn about it. I sent her a book to read hoping to get her pointed in the right direction. She tried to be supportive and initially we spoke often, but the calls tapered off and, similar to John's own mother, didn't always ask about John and how he was doing. I realize now that they probably just didn't know what to say or how to bring up the subject. Maybe they thought that if anything bad happened then I would let them know, but that's wasn't the case. If they didn't ask, I didn't tell. Most of the time I thought they only wanted to hear the good news and not any bad news.

Within a few weeks, John started to feel better and the depression lifted. At John's next appointment, the doctor decided to battle some of the unwanted side effects that were still present. Therefore, Dr. G. increased the *Risperidone* to three milligrams believing these side effects were attributed to the illness rather than the medication. John wasn't thrilled about the increased dosage but was definitely willing to try.

One month later, the disorganization and concentration hadn't improved and both John and Dr. G. weren't satisfied with that. John wanted to be back at work in a fully productive manner and wasn't willing to accept anything less. He was very determined and optimistic that he could get there. The doctor added another type of antidepressant to the mix called *Wellbutrin,* hoping John would gain some mental clarity with this drug and would focus better. John didn't notice much of a difference after one month of taking it and at the next appointment Dr. G. doubled the dose of *Wellbutrin.*

What we have learned to date is that in order to keep the delusions away and for John to feel good, we have to find the correct balance of medications. Achieving that balance takes extended periods of time and patience. Every person is different and each person's body chemistry reacts differently with each medication. Only once did John ever mention that he wanted to quit taking his medications so his mind would clear and he could work again but he is also aware that Delusional John will return. Therefore, there really isn't a choice for him.

Schizophrenia is the most severe mental illness of the mind and affects one percent of the Canadian population. John hasn't been able to work effectively for almost a year now. Subsequently, neither have I. I feel what John feels. I suffer everything he suffers. I am scared to make a sales call. I am afraid of triggering another psychotic episode. I don't know if that's possible or not but right now, I am not willing to take the chance. I won't do anything that will jeopardize John's recovery. I have a hard time concentrating on my own work because I am so preoccupied with John that it doesn't leave room for much else. I am constantly looking for new journal articles and reading books about schizophrenia and mental illness. Books for the patient, books for the families, medical books and memoirs. I want to learn as much as I can about this dreaded illness.

This whole experience is very frustrating for John and all he wants is to get back to work. I am constantly amazed at his composure and optimism. Not once has he wallowed in self-pity, unlike me, or moped around the house feeling sorry for himself, unlike me. John holds a responsible position at work and has a number of people working with him in his group. He is a program leader and can't lead anything right now. The fear that he won't be able to return to work in the same capacity is traumatic and causes him an enormous amount of stress and stress isn't good for him. Stress can trigger new psychotic events.

After being on antipsychotic medication for over nine months now, John has also developed another side effect from the drugs called Tardive Dyskinesia. This means John has involuntary muscular movements similar to some patients with Parkinson's illness. John often looks like he is chewing on a tiny piece of gum making his chin move up and down and his lips move. At times, he gets rapid eye blinking and has no awareness of it. These movements are involuntary and he doesn't notice it happening until one of the kids or I mention it. I have read that these symptoms may or may not disappear over time but often are non-reversible. I suppose this is a small concession for a delusional-free husband. At home, it doesn't matter how much he blinks or smacks his jaw about, but if the symptom persists or worsens, John would feel self-conscious about it at work or while out in public. Also this side effect is sometimes irreversible.

Often John stares off into space and looks deep in thought. He is sometimes oblivious to what is happening in the house and seems disengaged much of the time. I forgot to set my alarm clock the night before school started and even though John was awake, he let the rest of us sleep in. He was focused on something else not thinking about anyone else at the time. When I asked him why he didn't wake us up, he didn't have an answer. He said he was thinking about other things.

He loses concentration easily and his mind can wander off in mid-conversation. It's hard for me to see John like this because before this illness he was usually very attentive and sharp. Multitasking was not difficult for John and now it is. He gets overwhelmed easily. He used to find it hard to watch the television but that is getting better as his concentration improves. John likes to read but writing, which is a large part of his job, is very difficult for him. He especially finds it hard to organize himself and focus. When John feels the urge to tell his colleagues or his boss about his illness, he gets anxious and doesn't know if he will ever be ready to let anyone know. So far, we have told very few people and John hasn't decided if he will ever be ready to tell. That will be John's choice and I respect his wishes as my husband and a respected researcher in his scientific and academic communities.

John's mom came to visit him in August, ten months after he first called the police to tell them he thought he was poisoned. We had a nice visit but she didn't seem to want to talk directly to John about his illness or anything that he experienced over the last several months. John's brothers call occasionally to talk to him and see how he is doing. We do appreciate their concern. John appreciates that they are busy with their work and their families.

Thinking about our future and all the many "what-if's" that may happen in our life is agonizing. What happens if John's colleagues find out about his illness? What happens if John can't work? We both know I don't have the earning potential that John has and could never support our household the way we live now. What happens if the medication stops working? What happens if the delusions return? What if John gets violent towards me or the kids? What if John doesn't want to take the medications any more? The list is endless and I get exhausted thinking about all these what-ifs. It is way too easy to let these types of thoughts spin out of control and I find myself tormented much of the time. The worst what-if I have, the one that keeps me awake most nights is: what if one of our children inherits this illness? From all that I have read I know there is a higher probability that one of the kids may have this illness too. For a mother, this is scary and worries me almost more than I can bear.

Is our society open-minded enough to accept someone who suffers from mental illness as the same as everyone else? We like to believe we treat people who have a physical disability as an able-bodied person who is capable but how do we treat people knowing there is something wrong with their mind? Do managers hire people who declare on their employment application that they have schizophrenia? When we see the big scary "S' word, do we immediately envision gruesome headlines or crazy, homeless street people muttering to themselves, palms up wanting our spare change?

Recent research shows that most violent crimes are not committed by persons with mental illnesses yet we hang on to that perception. For this, we can blame the media which love to report these tragic stories but often fail to include important details such as the fact that the offenders suffered from an untreated mental illness or were off their meds at the time. From everything I have learned about this illness, schizophrenia has the worst reputation and gets a really bad rap. The discrimination people suffer has a very real, negative impact on the lives of those already suffering. Who breaks the stereotype?

When do people like John get a break? He has been very compliant. He vigilantly takes his medication every day. He attends all his doctor's appointments. He is trying to get better. When do people with a mental illness not have to worry about what other people are thinking about them and endure the whispering behind their backs?

If I decide to change the names and some of the identifying events in this story to protect our identities, and am lucky enough to find a publisher who is willing to publish this story, am I being a hypocrite? Am I encouraging the mental illness stereotype? I wonder how ready our society is to accept that one in one hundred people suffer from a severe mental illness and one in five people will suffer from some form of a mental illness at some point in their life. We all probably know someone who has some form of mental illness and just don't realize they do. It is very prevalent in our society, yet no one wants to talk about it.

So why did I write this book then? I wrote this book for my children so that even though they lived and suffered through their father's illness, they will have an accurate account and know the truth of what happened to them at this time in their life. This illness affected our whole family and the events of the last year will be a part of them. It will affect them and if they have any questions, they will know where to find the answers. We kept our two older children in the loop as much as possible and were very truthful about what happened. They seemed to have processed it well and are doing great. We told our youngest that Dad has a sickness that affects his brain called schizophrenia. He takes medication to control it and make him better. Sam asked if the medication locks the illness away with a key and then the key gets thrown away and we said, "Yes!"

I want the descendants of this family to know this story too. If any of them sadly happen to experience delusions, hallucinations or voices in their heads, then knowing this story will hopefully give them the courage and strength to seek help. It may help them understand themselves a little better. Maybe it will be a tiny bit less scary if they know something about mental illness beforehand. Certainly knowing it exists in the family will provide them and their doctors with a place to start.

For anyone else that reads this story, maybe you will have gained the experience and knowledge of a mental illness without having to live through it. I would not wish that on anyone. Optimistically, I hope our story will provide tolerance and understanding about mental illness and that it can happen to anyone. It is an illness that does not discriminate amongst gender, race or age. If only one person reads this, then perhaps we are one step closer to breaking the social stigma of mental illness. It is alright to talk about it. This isn't something we need to be embarrassed about and sweep under the carpet as if it didn't exist. Mental illness is real and can be treated, beginning with a willingness to accept it. It is not a sign of weakness or a disease reserved for the lazy people in this world. There is no shame in suffering from mental illness.

Chapter 17 - Reflection

Here is where my story finishes even though I don't know how it ends yet. Every morning is a struggle for me to face what's happened to us and I have to force myself to accept this illness in order to get out of bed each day. I wish I had John's optimism and good nature. If I can't have that, then I wish I had some of his drugs.

I no longer wish John had some other, terrible illness like cancer. That's just wrong. I still feel our future is on hold and we are waiting around to see what will happen. Waiting is both agonizing and depressing; therefore, we don't talk about our future very often. I still watch John like a jack-in-the-box anticipating his next move, never knowing if Delusional John will pop out.

I am always aware of his illness and know a break-through event can occur—a return of his delusions. I am not ready to trust the medication one hundred percent. At any given moment, John's illness could gain momentum and Delusional John could show up unannounced. The next time that monster shows up, I am armed and I am ready. I have knowledge and I have experience. I am prepared.

John's personality is different now that he has been on the medication, and it can be challenging at times. I dearly miss the man I once relied on so heavily for comfort and joy. I miss my lover and my best friend. I have become the one who was taken care of, to the one doing the care taking. That in itself isn't such a burden or hard work; it's just that I was not expecting this. I miss John showing up unexpectedly with a bouquet of flowers. I miss little things like trying out a new recipe together and shopping for that perfect bottle of red wine to go with it. I miss having a drink on a Saturday night and listening to music while ignoring the kids. I miss entertaining and having friends over. I miss the intimacy and the pillow talk. I miss the energy and enthusiasm for life that we once shared. I miss the happy. Dealing with this illness has been a very lonely experience, even though I am not alone. The bond between John and me is solid and stronger than it ever has been. We know exactly what we mean to each other and know that we can survive anything. There are no regrets.

So how are things now? It's not all doom and gloom. I love my husband with all my heart. I am filled with so much pride for him. I admire his courage and strength, and I am in awe of his positive attitude. I appreciate his determination, his willingness to carry on and not give up. He has stood up tall every day and challenged this illness and constantly fights to put his life back together. He always says it could be worse and that is so true. We are still together and working on getting our happy back.

I am still in love with my husband and just as honoured to be his wife today as was the day I married him. When I look into his face, I do not see a man with schizophrenia. I see an intelligent man driven to succeed. I see a man who would do anything to protect his family.

There is nothing more important to John than the kids and I. He works hard at getting better because he has so much at stake.

When I look into John's beautiful eyes, I see love looking back at me. The crazy eyes have long gone away. When I think about what our children have inherited from their father, being scared for them isn't the first thing I think about anymore. I think about the exceptional qualities that he has passed to them like courage, kindness, tenacity and generosity, for these are the qualities we believe that determine success and happiness in this life. I will not let this illness define the future of our children.

I have to learn to accept this horrible illness rather than spend all my time and energy fighting it. I need to work through the grief and anguish this illness has brought to our family. No one knows what causes schizophrenia but I am hopeful that medical researchers will figure it out one day. I too, in time, will rise to the challenge and learn to work around it.

Knowing John is not the same man is painful. Every day I pick-up a piece or two from our old life and place it into our new life. Mostly every day is better than the day before. Sometimes it's not and we have to work at it but most days are good.

John smiles more now and his sense of humour is returning. We are able to laugh at each other's jokes. There are times during the day where one or both of us are happy, even if is just for a few moments. Our dreams and our future are waiting for us somewhere out there, we just need to wait a little while and then go after them. John is still the same kind, loving man I fell deeply in love with all those years ago and together we will learn to cope. We will embrace our life together and we will be happy again. This is a love story after all.

John and Marion 2012

Chapter 18 – Where We're At Now

Almost one year later, John has continued to improve remarkably. After being very stable for an entire year and taking his medication faithfully everyday, the doctor has reduced John's antipsychotic medication significantly and removed one of the antidepressants completely. We try to eat healthy, exercise, get plenty of sleep and we both have remained healthy for the past year. We have escaped seasonal flu, no colds and no other illnesses. We consider ourselves lucky.

I resigned from my family business at the end of 2012 and am back to running my own home daycare business. It is less stressful for me and spending my days with babies is a wonderful way to earn an income. Working from home also allows me to be available for our own children and John if they need me. They are all on board and supportive of my career change and enjoy the babies also. It wouldn't work if they were not accommodating; our home has been transformed into a daycare. The boys each have a playpen in their room for the babies' naps and our family room has become the playroom. The kitchen eating area is now crowded by three highchairs. At the time I am writing this I have not informed the parents whose children I take care of about John's illness and very soon the time will come when I will have to tell them. I don't want this to come as a surprise or considered a secret to be ashamed of because it is not. John was ill, he is on medication and now he is better. It shouldn't be a big deal letting them know, yet I still worry about it. Will they pull their children from my care? Will they be upset I didn't inform them from the beginning? I will find out soon enough.

Our daughter left for the University of Toronto in the fall of 2012 and is enjoying her time away at school. I miss her every day but also know that she has a job to do and that is where she belongs. We try to talk and text each other as much as we can and have remained close. Our boys are doing well and for the most part our life has settled down and we are back to a regular routine and a simpler life.

John still does not have a psychiatrist that he can visit for ongoing care nor will he get one. Our health care system does not allow for such luxurious resources. John isn't sick enough to warrant ongoing psychiatric care. Knowing this has somewhat lessened the agony of waiting, at least in this area.

John's doctor still has not committed to schizophrenia as the final diagnosis. He told John he didn't think he could be functioning and working at the capacity in which he does if it were schizophrenia. The doctor suggested perhaps a mild form of schizophrenia mixed with something else, maybe bipolar disorder. We are not so sure we agree with that but are not in a position to argue with the doctor since he is the only one providing John with the care he is receiving, psychiatric or otherwise. We do appreciate the doctor's willingness to experiment with the medications and understand the limitations of his experience and knowledge in psychiatric care. John was pleased when the doctor agreed to reduce the Risperidone dosage and felt the effects almost immediately. Sitting in front of the fire, enjoying a glass of wine together one evening, John unexpectedly told me that he thought he was having an emotional awakening of sorts. He could feel the difference the lowered dosage was having. It made me worry that he was also going to reconsider the publication of the book. Maybe he didn't care I was publishing because the medication handcuffed the emotional side of himself and now he was having second thoughts. Uh-oh, I had already signed the contract. Luckily this was not the case and John still believes that this book can help other people going through similar circumstances. More importantly, John does not want to teach the kids that this is something to hide from or feel ashamed about.

We have kind of shelved the idea of getting a firm diagnosis for a few reasons. First, we have learned that diagnosing a mental illness is very tricky business and realistically it can take years. I know that sounds extreme but it is true. Secondly, John has responded so well to the right medication and that is what is important. Things could be so much worse. I have heard about people and read first hand stories about individuals who have been hospitalized numerous times and had brushes with the law. Others have been unable to work for months and their once promising careers have been altered or redirected. Still others have yet to find the right balance or type of medication that is effective or even worse, find they are medication resistant. Sadly, there are also those who refuse to take any medication or won't accept the idea that they are mentally ill. Whatever the correct diagnosis is, John is doing very well and the medication is working. He has been delusion free for over a year and is ready to let people know about his illness. It was his idea that I seek a publisher and he willingly wrote about his delusional experiences to include in this book. When I offered to change the names and any identifying information, John refused. Knowing this story wouldn't help anyone if we weren't willing to say who we are and would only add to the negative stigma that already persists.

Very recently, we have both told a few people about John's illness and there has been a mixed response ranging from support and compassion to indifference. Sometimes, the reaction I was expecting is not what I received. I have learned not to expect anything and therefore cannot be disappointed but only pleasantly surprised. Mental illness is not treated like other illnesses such as cancer, heart disease or diabetes. During the times when John was in the hospital and the months he spent at home unable to work, no one sent cards, there were no flowers and very few phone calls from anyone wanting to talk to John. That is just so sad.

Hearing the words mental illness or schizophrenia evokes fear in people mostly because they are not familiar with these types of illness. Schizophrenia is perhaps the most severe mental illness a person can have and it is also one of the most misunderstood illnesses. Not knowing enough about the illness is scary but it doesn't have to be. We have published this book and told our story to help people understand mental illness a little better and tell you that it is not something to be afraid of. Having a mental illness is not a character flaw. It is not something you come down with because you are lazy, unmotivated or haven't prayed hard enough. Not all mentally people are violent and only some violent people are mentally ill. Except for the first night when I barricaded our front door with the

166

love-seat I was never scared of John. I never felt afraid he would physically harm me or the kids. He simply is not a violent person. What I am scared of is that our marriage is not strong enough to outlast the recovery time of the illness. Sometimes, I am afraid we might not make it. I have not forgotten all the terrible things John accused me of but I have forgiven him. It is not his fault; he was sick. I am reminded constantly of what happened and it is a struggle for me to keep moving past it, but it is getting easier. I am working through the grief with the help of a counsellor and a support group. I certainly have come to terms with everything much better and feel stronger. At what point does John's recovery turn into "recovered" and will it leave our marriage in a place that we are happy with each other and can carry on? I can't wait to find out and I have a pretty good feeling that it will.

It has been a humbling experience learning to live with this larger-than-life illness so present in our lives. I am so much more aware and empathetic to what other people may have going on in their lives. But what is even larger than the illness is the stigma attached to it. The media are largely responsible for reinforcing negative stigma but have the opportunity to change. People that are afflicted with these terrible illnesses need compassion and understanding. They need the support of the friends and family at a time in their life where their future appears bleak, desperate and hopeless. Reporting incidents where a mentally ill person harms another person is utterly irresponsible and reckless and should not be considered newsworthy. The media have the opportunity to report how badly the mentally ill are mismanaged. The lack of funding and allotted resources should be brought to the attention of the public instead of tragic individual isolated cases.

John and I have become sensitive when we hear people use the word "schizophrenia" loosely or refer to someone as being schizophrenic, bipolar or crazy without knowing their diagnosis. Using slang words like "schizoid" or "schizo" is rude and reinforces the negative stigma attached to this illness. The stigma attached to mental illness is so great that it often prevents an ill person from seeking help. Who wants to admit to having an illness when you feel you would damage your reputation, lose your job, or be alienated from your friends and family? How sad is that? A survey conducted by the *Globe and Mail* in 2008, only five years ago, indicated that forty-two percent of the people surveyed would no longer socialize with a friend diagnosed with a mental illness! Wow! Well it's time to break the silence, speak out and erase the stigma.

This book will come as a surprise and maybe even shock some friends and family members. Only a small number of people know. My apology goes out to those whom we have surprised or shocked. Many of the details are shocking, we know. There is no rule book on what to do in a situation like this. We did what we did in order to survive.

Afterword, Dr David Dawson

I am always surprised and distressed by the poor quality of psychiatric care documented in this and many other family and first-person accounts, though I am not surprised by the diagnostic confusion.

A man or woman, educated, employed, married with children, becomes delusional. This is as serious and portentous an illness as a malignancy, heart failure, or type I diabetes. It should receive the same attention, the same degree of urgent care, the same degree of follow-up and aftercare. It should warrant the same degree of specialized attention, of access to a specialist. And the care received should be as transparent and comprehensive as that found in modern day oncology.

For that matter this same level of good care should be available to a man or woman who is not educated, not married, not employed, who becomes delusional.

Attitudes about mental illness, stigma, and limited resources play roles in this failure, but then so do the symptoms of mental illness. Most of us have ways, now, of understanding the words "cancer", "malignant", "metastases", "heart failure", "diabetes" – but what of the words "delusional", "psychotic"?

And if we understand schizophrenia as being an illness that begins in adolescence, how do we explain someone who achieved a PhD, who courted, and married, and had children, who found employment in responsible positions in several countries, who seemed perfectly well and sane into his late twenties and then and only then developed symptoms of this illness?

It is easy enough, I think, to understand a malignant cancer cell and heart failure, because we understand what ordinary cells do and what the heart does. Our cells divide and replace themselves in a controlled fashion and they don't intrude on other cells, nor do they usually take root where they are unwanted. In this fashion our bodies rebuild themselves without greatly changing beyond all those minor failings we call aging. We know what our cells should be doing, and so when kidney cells are found growing into a bone we know that is wrong and dangerous and we call it cancer. We know and can picture in our minds how hearts work and what they are supposed to do, so we understand when that muscle weakens and can no longer pump hard enough to move our blood and we begin to fill with fluid where we shouldn't be filling with fluid, that that is wrong, and we call it heart failure.

But what of the brain, a far more complicated organ, made even more complicated by our insistence on believing in some kind of mind, of a consciousness or being that is somehow separate from the physical components of the brain? How can we understand delusion, the concept of delusion, a thought or conviction not based on reality, when we are perfectly willing to accept a thought or conviction based on a belief in what Bill Maher calls "an imaginary friend"?

And while we can grasp the dynamics, the cause effect relationship of a failing heart muscle and fluid retention, how might we understand or make the link from some component of the brain failing with such a complex outcome as a conviction that "the police are following me and controlling me with radio waves."

Our psychiatric diagnostic systems are not there yet. They are our best and always evolving ways of categorizing clusters of symptoms, natural courses of these symptoms, and their response to treatment. We cannot yet delineate the specific causes, the parts of the brain affected, and the pathways that lead to those most confusing and perplexing of symptoms.

Which is all the more reason why, if we cannot label something in a sure and useful fashion, we should spend even more time explaining what we know and what we don't know to our patients and their families.

Here is a way of understanding delusions:

As human beings, we, as directed by our brains, operate with certain imperatives. We have desires and hungers we seek to satisfy. We respond to and avoid pain. We (at least once we are past our adolescence) seek to avoid death. As with other primates we organize in families and tribes. As with bees and ants we may even have some altruistic impulses. And as with our cousins the chimpanzees we seek out, we learn, and keep vigilant to threats, to safe havens, to nest building and protecting, and remain alert always to whom we may control and who may control us. To do this, the chimpanzee must maintain some kind of map in his head, some graph, some kind of symbolic representation. And we do the same. But unlike the chimpanzee we put words to this symbolic representation, and abstract thought, metaphors and similes.

In short, we are driven to always understand the world around us and our place in it. And the parameters our brains must satisfy are the same ones our primate cousins must satisfy: Power, control, threat, safety, love, kinship, and sex. And while our primate cousins' mental map of power and control ends at one pole with the current Alpha Male, our mental map includes the possibility of a "higher power" or invisible alpha male.

We have one other sophistication above that of our primate cousins; we are adaptable. We can more easily adapt to changes in social status, to environment, to new and novel situations.

We don't fully understand the parts of the brain involved in this process, but we know it involves non-textual communication and it starts very early, with the first smile exchanged between infant and mother, and goes on to the greatest test to our social adaptability occurring in adolescence and early adulthood. Throughout this our brains function with an imperative of organizing, of mapping, of finding a way of understanding our place in this social world.

Now if the imperative remains, but those parts of the brain that normally satisfy that imperative begin to fail, be it through a neurohormone failure or failed connections, a blow to the head, a toxic insult, the brain must still satisfy its hunger for organizing, for mapping, its need for predictability. It still needs to know where it stands with respect to power, control, threat, safety, love, kinship and sex within its social world. And if it cannot discern the patterns and structures through an ordinary process of communication, nonverbal and verbal, then it will invent such patterns. And these invented patterns always provide answers to the questions of power (including God), control, threat, safety, love, kinship, and sex.

But we humans are nothing if not resourceful. We compensate for our deficits. We avoid that which gives us grief and confusion. And if we are intellectually gifted, adept at language use and abstract thought, we may use these to hold the chaos at bay along with false and invented maps, for as long as we possibly can. But the imperative persists. The world becomes more, not less complex, until finally an event, a coincidence, a strong feeling or a loss triggers a cascade of delusional ideas.

It is the same disease suffered by the teen who hides in the bedroom of his parents' home, and looking back there were always warning signs, but it has occurred only now because a gifted intellect was able to hold it at bay within a stable loving relationship.

There is a scene in *A Beautiful Mind* that stands out: As a graduate student Mr. Nash is in a bar with colleagues when some women enter. As with all our primate cousins the male brain begins immediately to work out ways to single out and meet and court and have sex with at least one of the women. For most of us, body posture, facial expression, the dance of eye contact will contain all the navigational tools we need. John Nash could not do this. He had schizophrenia. He had lost this ability. But what he could do was apply his very own, highly intellectual and textually dependent Game Theory to the problem.

Dr Dawson was formerly a Professor of Psychiatry at McMaster University and psychiatrist in chief of the Hamilton (ON, Canada) Psychiatric Hospital. He now works part-time in clinical psychiatry primarily with families, children and adolescents. The rest of the time is devoted to teaching, art, writing and film making. He is the author of two academic books and a number of trade books – both fiction and non-fiction. He also writes and directs films

SIMILAR TITLES FROM BRIDGEROSS

Schizophrenia Medicine's Mystery Society's Shame by Marvin Ross - recommended by the World Fellowship for Schizophrenia and Allied Disorders. "a powerful resource for anyone looking for answers and insight into the world of mental illness." Schizophrenia Digest Magazine, Fall 2008

After Her Brain Broke: Helping My Daughter Recover Her Sanity, by Susan Inman. A poignant memoir describing the family's nine year journey to help her younger daughter recover from a catastrophic schizoaffective disorder and recommended by NAMI.

My Schizophrenic Life: The Road to Recovery From Mental Illness by Sandra Yuen MacKay. "Inspirational and fosters some hope for recovery" , Canadian Journal of Occupational Therapy; "remarkably compelling", Library Journal and recommended by NAMI

What A Life Can Be: One Therapist's Take on Schizo-affective Disorder, by Carolyn Dobbins, PhD "powerful and revealing, and provides a unique insight into chronic mental disease" Dr. Thomas G Burish, a professor of psychology and Provost of Notre Dame.

When Quietness Came: A Neuroscientist's Personal Journey With Schizophrenia, by Erin Hawkes, MSc. The true story of a young woman studying neuroscience who, in her final undergraduate year, has a psychotic break, attempts suicide and ends up in hospital. Her struggles to get well and to pursue her PhD are described.

Love's All That Makes Sense A Mother Daughter Memoir by Sakeenah and Anika Francis. Growing up with a mother with schizophrenia as told by both from their own unique perspectives

The Brush, The Pen and Recovery, A 33 minute documentary film on an art program for people with schizophrenia,

Schizophrenia In Focus, A 54 minute documentary created by psychiatrist and filmmaker David Laing Dawson.

CPSIA information can be obtained
at www.ICGtesting.com
Printed in the USA
FFOW02n0859270914
7603FF